WILDERNESS CAMPING
in the
ADIRONDACKS

25 Backpacking and Canoeing Overnight Adventures

BILL INGERSOLL

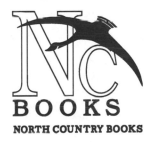

BOOKS

NORTH COUNTRY BOOKS

An imprint of Globe Pequot, the trade division of
The Rowman & Littlefield Publishing Group, Inc.
4501 Forbes Blvd., Ste. 200
Lanham, MD 20706
www.rowman.com

Distributed by NATIONAL BOOK NETWORK

British Library Cataloguing in Publication Information Available

Library of Congress Cataloging-in-Publication Data

Names: Ingersoll, Bill, author.
Title: Wilderness camping in the Adirondacks : 25 hiking and canoeing]overnight adventures /
    Bill Ingersoll.
Description: Lanham, MD : Government Institutes, 2024. | Includes index. | Summary: "With
    detailed trail and waterway maps for each Adirondacks is the perfect companion to any
    weekend getaway or multinight journey in the lakes, mountains, rivers, and trails of the
    Adirondacks"—Provided by publisher.
Identifiers: LCCN 2023045057 (print) | LCCN 2023045058 (ebook) | ISBN 9781493080946
    (paperback) | ISBN 9781493080953 (epub)
Subjects: LCSH: Camping—New York (State)—Adirondack Mountains—Guidebooks. | Trails—
    New York (State)—Adirondack Mountains—Guidebooks. | Hiking—New York (State)—
    Adirondack Mountains—Guidebooks. | Canoes and canoeing—New York (State)—
    Adirondack Mountains—Guidebooks. | Adirondack Mountains (N.Y.)—Guidebooks. | BISAC:
    SPORTS & RECREATION / Camping | SPORTS & RECREATION / Water Sports / Canoeing
Classification: LCC GV191.42.N7 I65 2024 (print) | LCC GV191.42.N7 (ebook) | DDC
    796.54/097475—dc23/eng/20231026
LC record available at https://lccn.loc.gov/2023045057
LC ebook record available at https://lccn.loc.gov/2023045058

CONTENTS

Map Legend

87 Interstate	Boat Launch
9 US Highway	Campground
28 State Highway	Lodging
CR1 County Road	Parking
Local Road	Point of Interest/Building
Improved Gravel Road	Peak/Summit
Trail	Restrooms
Featured Route	Tower
Railroad	Trailhead
Wilderness/Park	Viewpoint/Overlook
	River or Creek
	Body of Water
	Marsh

INTRODUCTION

When many outdoor-loving people rattle off lists of their favorite wilderness landscapes, Adirondack Park often gets short shrift as though people are biased against its state park designation. How can such a place compare to something as grandiose as the Grand Canyon or Yosemite? If the place was really any good, wouldn't they charge an entry fee just to get in?

Or there are the people who are simply not familiar with the geography of our state—who perhaps think, for instance, that when I speak of "northern New York" I am referring to the general vicinity of Yankee Stadium.

"Preposterous!" they jeer. "Maine, maybe, but New York? How could you even squeeze in twenty-five wilderness campsites between all those delis and subway stations?"

Ah, but the joke is on the people who equate "national" with "superior," or who find it difficult to believe that any of the experiences described in this book are possible in the Empire State. Don't get me wrong—the national parks are outstanding. I know, because I've been to a few of them. But I also know that Adirondack Park is every bit as good. If it's lacking in mile-deep canyons or sheer granite cliffs, it abounds in sheer . . . abundance. Bigger than some states, it is an ocean of wilderness where most people probably expect to find golf courses and subdivisions.

Indeed, the hardest part about writing this guidebook was picking the twenty-five routes I wanted to include. Out of plenty, I had to select just a few, winnowing down the seemingly endless camping options to a relatively slender menu of trails and waterways—a guide book big enough for a 6-million-acre park, but small enough to stow in a backpack.

Hopefully you are more like me and already have some familiarity with the place. I suspect you're an insider. Possibly you know the Adirondacks quite well, and now you're looking to explore the wilder side of the park.

If so, this book is intended to be an introductory resource that (if I did my job well) will start you off along the same path that I've been experiencing ever since I first got hooked on the Adirondacks myself. The outings that I have selected were chosen for multiple reasons, the chief one being that all lead to good wilderness camping destinations, of course. But this is not a bucket list, something to be hurriedly checked off before you die. Rather, I hope each of these overnight trips will help provide instruction on how to live. There is, after all, more to the human existence than just touchscreens and takeout. A good campfire on a cool, starlit night counts for something, too.

None of the recommended outings in this book require a super investment of time or a wealth of outdoor skill. All one really needs is the curiosity and the wherewithal to explore some new-to-you places, as well as the ability to swing a few free weekends to make these adventures happen. As you progress you may very well outgrow this book and advance to the more difficult-to-find places. But even if you systematically execute all twenty-five camping trips exactly as I've described them, you will still feel like you've been somewhere. There isn't one in the bunch I haven't done myself.

The obvious place to begin is with the basics: What is Adirondack Park, and why should you want to explore it? But before I get into the details, I'll explain instead what the Adirondacks are to me:

They are a bushwhack up a little-known mountain with the most photogenic view imaginable of places most people have never heard about.

They are a winding river that today seems populated by no one but me, the dog sitting in the front of my canoe, and the otter that acts outraged over our intrusion.

They are a night spent camping beside a remote lake, falling asleep to the echoing wail of a loon.

They are the surprise encounter with a bull moose feeding on lily pads, in the shallows just off the shore of a lake—the name of which I refuse to disclose to anyone without a need-to-know basis.

They are a mountain slope cloaked in a burning display of red foliage, peaking during the fleetest of windows in early October.

They are the remote waterfall that I have all to myself for an entire weekend—the only person out of a global population of billions who chose to be at this place, at this time.

What Are the Adirondacks?

Explanations for why the Adirondack Mountains exist where they do and how they do are few and far between. This is not some offshoot of the nearby Appalachians, the stubby remnants of a forgotten continental collision. Our mountains are something different, a round range spewing rivers in every conceivable direction, not readily anticipated by a schoolbook understanding of tectonic theory.

What we do know is that the Adirondacks are relatively new peaks made out of extremely old rocks. Whereas most mountains are eroding and slowly getting smaller, the summits of the Adirondacks are still rising. According to my lay understanding of current advancements in geology, the North American Plate is drifting over the fragmented remains of another lost plate, one which was subducted hundreds of millions of years ago off the West Coast and is now slowly being recycled within the Earth's mantle. Some of the pieces of this literal lost continent are lifting up various other parts of North America like Hadean speedbumps—the Adirondacks perhaps among them.

Whatever the cause, mountains in the Adirondacks are scattered in a nearly random arrangement across the landscape, not in compressed and craggy strings in the manner of most mountain ranges. No continental fault lines lie anywhere nearby, and rivers flow off the plateau in whichever compass direction they please. This is less of a tectonic dividing line than a regional anomaly.

Nor is this merely a mountain range. The park is dotted with lakes, ponds, and bogs of every size, and these watery features are just as "Adirondack" as the mountains and the trees. Some lakes are shallow and warm; a few ponds are high and frigid. Streams connect them all. Therefore from a human-powered recreation point of view, not only is this a park to explore on foot, but one that also screams that you should bring a paddle.

View from Weston Mountain. *Photo courtesy of the author*

The region we now call the Adirondacks was slow to accept human habitation. The earliest European settlers avoided the place, and some colonial maps depicted it has a nameless void filled with miasmic swamps and other unpleasantries. Certainly the Native American nations knew these mountains and forests very well; they traversed the wilderness on well-worn trails and reportedly skirmished with their enemies here. A few sites labeled as "Indian Clearings," though mostly now forgotten, hint at periods of occupation. When European couture developed a taste for felt hats made from beaver fur, this was one of the places Indians and other trappers depleted of those rodents at a fairly early date.

Few colonists understood the mountains, but that didn't stop some from claiming to own them. In a process that began before the Revolutionary War, land agents working on behalf of the British crown negotiated lopsided land purchases with the Iroquois, whose Haudenosaunee Confederacy once claimed supremacy from the Mohawk to the St. Lawrence and beyond. After the war, the new State of New York assumed possession of the wilderness at a time when the sheer abundance of land was its primary source of economic wealth.

Settlement did penetrate the fringes of the mountains as early as the 1790s, with other successful communities springing up along the Sacandaga River and west of Lake Champlain in the opening decades of the nineteenth century. But even the hardiest people had mixed feelings about the deep interior. Hamilton County, which today exists entirely within Adirondack Park, was founded with enthusiasm but never quite grew as planned. People of the day, giddy with the prospect of cheap land, wanted nothing more than a self-sufficient farm, and frankly there were more fertile fields elsewhere.

But even as this lukewarm attempt to civilize the wilderness began to take hold, scientific knowledge of the region arrived late. The first geographic expedition into the mountains did not occur until 1837. This was more than three decades after Lewis and Clark!

Nor did the region have a formal name. Up until 1837 people referred to the mountains and the surrounding wilderness by different appellations: it was the Great North Woods to people living to the south, or the Great South Woods from the perspective of people in St. Lawrence County, and John Brown's Tract for people entering from the southwest. The leaders of the 1837 expedition chose the name "Adirondack," but just for the highest range of mountains at the center of the forest, known today as the High Peaks. They claimed to be honoring a lost Indian nation once believed to inhabit the region, although not much else is known about those people other than the name

Things changed after the Civil War, by which time the state's railroad system was beginning to make outdoor tourism more feasible. No lines ran into the mountains (at first), but they did service the peripheral valleys, from whence it was possible to follow the primitive road system upcountry for a summer's worth of adventures.

And did the people come! The final decades of the nineteenth century are remembered as a nostalgic heyday, even though the wooden hotels were frequently burning down and game laws were nonexistent. "Sports" hired guides to row them into the Adirondack wilderness, which they perceived as a sylvan land of plenty. They took pleasure in activities that would make today's outdoor explorers squirm: jacking deer at night simply because they could, shooting loons to keep the lakes quiet, peeling sheets of bark off of live trees to make a temporary shelter.

Nevertheless a cultural aesthetic was born, and public interest in the wild potential of the Adirondacks was ignited. That flame has only ever grown brighter since.

At the same time, the rate of logging was increasing. You will hear many people today repeat the same fiction that the Adirondacks were denuded of trees by a rapacious forest industry, and that was why the region was later protected as a park. It's a good story, but things didn't quite happen that way. In reality these woods were so remote and difficult to reach that the loggers favored only a handful of tree species—particularly those that could be floated down the major rivers to the waiting sawmills. Mostly it was the areas nearest the settlements that were cleared, either for agriculture or for charcoal production. Sometimes both.

Engineers in the employ of the state's Canal Board took a keen interest in the region's abundant water resources as early as the 1840s, however. New York's economic preeminence was based in part on the success of the Erie Canal and its various branches, which required steady sources of water. This became the impetus for the original idea of creating a park: people were beginning to piece together the relationship between a healthy forest and a healthy watershed; therefore, to preserve one was to save the other.

Thus when the fear of over-logging became married to the idea of sustaining the state's water wealth—that a deforested landscape would become desiccated, turning an environmental disaster into an economic one—people began to think in terms of protecting the Adirondacks as a park.

This development occurred in stages. The first act was the creation of the Forest Preserve in 1885, which made it a crime to destroy timber on those Adirondack lands owned by the state. This was a significant but preliminary achievement, since by then the state's holdings consisted only of scattered small holdings all over the mountains, many of them acquired when various lumber interests defaulted on their property taxes after removing the merchantable timber.

The next major step was the creation of Adirondack Park itself in 1892. Delineated by a blue line on official maps, the park was significantly smaller at the time of inception than it is now. The "Blue Line" encircled the wildest, least-developed core acreage but excluded large areas to the east and north. Much of the region still remained privately owned; the designation was the state's way of signifying this was where its future land acquisitions would be prioritized.

The final significant act of the nineteenth century was the passage of Article VII, Section 7 as an amendment to the state's constitution in 1894. The so-called "forever wild clause" elevated the Forest Preserve laws from 1885, making the destruction of timber or the sale of state land a constitutional issue—essentially the highest form of legal protection available. Now renumbered Article XIV, this clause continues to guarantee no major changes can occur to Forest Preserve management without approval in a public referendum.

The twentieth century was a time of significant growth for both Adirondack Park and the Forest Preserve. The "Blue Line" grew on several occasions to encompass an area roughly twice as large as the original park, including not only the entire geological uplift area but also a portion of Lake Champlain, for a total of some 6 million acres.

At the same time, New York State continued to reacquire land. Although it had once owned the entire region, nearly all of the landscape (except the islands of Lake George) had long since been sold off as a source of revenue. But as the state's financial position matured, it was now able to invest significant funds into a land acquisition program that remains active to this day. The scattered parcels of the original Forest Preserve, numbering in the tens of thousands of acres, have grown to more than 3 million acres, including several significant tracts of contiguous wilderness.

This origin story for Adirondack Park, however, has had interesting implications. Unlike many of the western national parks, which were carved by Acts of Congress out of existing federal lands, entire municipalities have always existed within the Blue Line. This has never been a park where people were only allowed in as visitors; people live here, send their children to public schools funded on Forest Preserve tax assessments, and establish businesses in every sector from tourism to light manufacturing.

Today, Adirondack Park is best described as a special planning region within the state, administered jointly by the Department of Environmental Conservation (DEC), which oversees the day-to-day management of the Forest Preserve, and the Adirondack Park Agency, established in 1971 to represent the state's interest in regional planning for both public and private lands.

This book will focus on the wilder half of Adirondack Park, of course, but one cannot reach those areas without passing through the region's many hamlets and villages. It is this dichotomy of wilderness and culture, coexisting side by side, that helps make this park so distinctive.

About This Guidebook

Wilderness Camping in the Adirondacks is intended as an introduction to backpacking and canoe camping in the Adirondack Forest Preserve, providing a variety of route suggestions for people who are willing to hike or paddle a few miles into the backcountry for an exceptional overnight experience.

The twenty-five destinations are hardly exhaustive, but they are located throughout the park and highlight many of its most distinctive features, from mountains to waterways. The backpacking destinations—including lean-tos and primitive campsites—are all accessed from well-established trails that can be easily followed by anyone with a basic "woods sense." The paddling destinations are somewhat less specific, in that waterways in the Adirondacks often lead to a multitude of camping options; I will describe how to get to the lake or river, but rather than recommending a single campsite, I'll point out there may be dozens to choose from.

All of these routes were selected in part for their suitability as two-day camping trips, allowing you to get a taste for the art of wilderness camping in the Adirondacks. While you could stretch these outings out into longer expeditions if you wanted, these itineraries are designed for a single overnight. This is by no means intended as a list of the twenty-five best outings or the only camping opportunities. Rather, it is a compilation of relatively straightforward routes that offer a variety of wilderness experiences.

Each route description begins with a summary designed to give you an at-a-glance idea of what each trip involves. The elements of that summary include hiking distance, elevation change and vertical rise, paddling distance, and getting there.

Hiking Distance

For the backpacking trips, this is the total walking distance for a hike, from the trailhead to the campsite. All of my trail measurements were made independently using a handheld global positioning system (GPS) unit, and so the distances I give may vary slightly from other sources, or even from the trail signs you may encounter in the woods.

Although I do not estimate hiking time in this book (since every outing is expected to be two days long!), one can nevertheless make a reasonable guess. A typical hiking pace is 2 miles per hour on a well-maintained trail across typical terrain. This pace may slow to 1 mile per hour on steep and rugged slopes, or even increase to 3 miles per hour if the trail is wide and flat, but for me 2 miles per hour has always been a good benchmark.

With that in mind, a 3-mile hike can usually be completed in one and a half hours, and so forth. Individual paces may vary, so you may need to recalibrate these estimates for your own hiking style—perhaps padding some extra time for breaks, photography, and all those other diversions we employ while catching our breath.

Elevation Change and Vertical Rise

Few trails are flat. But while elevations in the Adirondacks are hardly as dramatic as those in mountain ranges out west, a long climb still makes a difference if you're chugging along with a heavy backpack. Therefore I provide these statistics as a way to gauge trail difficulty.

Vertical rise refers to the net elevation change from the trailhead to the highest point of the hike. For instance, if you park at 1,500 feet in elevation and hike to a lean-to at 2,200 feet, the vertical rise is 700 feet—the amount of uphill climbing you will need to complete.

Elevation change is the term I use for trails that have no particular end elevation in mind. Instead of climbing to an apex destination, many cross-country routes ascend and descend many minor hills en route to the campsite. Therefore this figure, when provided, represents the cumulative vertical rise and descent from the trailhead to the campsite.

However, many trails have too many trifling slopes, and these I simply describe as "rolling terrain." Granted, some of these hills may be noteworthy, and I will point out the presence of any especially steep climbs you should know about, but adding up the vertical rise of every single bump in the trail would simply lead to an inflated number that makes the overall route look more difficult than it really is.

Paddling Distance

For the canoe routes, distance is much more of a variable since canoes and kayaks aren't bound to a single path the way hiking boots are. Because all of the routes I've picked are waterbodies with multiple campsites—dozens in some cases—and because no one can predict one's actual path across a wide-open lake, these distances are mere guideposts. The best I can offer is the minimal distances from the launching point to the nearest and farthest campsites.

How you get from point A to point B will depend on a number of factors. On a calm day you may be able to paddle directly across an open lake, reaching your chosen campsite in the shortest distance possible. Or maybe a strong headwind will force you to take a more circuitous route that favors the leeward shoreline.

Either way, one of the joys of paddling in the Adirondacks is in following the shoreline, which is where the scenery is best (as are the opportunities to spot wildlife). Unless you are tracking your wandering path with a GPS—including every twist, turn, tack, and detour—your actual paddling distance will remain an unknown number.

Getting There

This section provides a narrative set of driving directions from the nearest town or major highway to the trailhead parking area. Often a trailhead will be located several miles down a seasonal access road in a remote location, capable of confounding even the most up-to-date GPS technology; therefore, these driving directions should be read as carefully as the route description itself. Note that many roads leading into the Forest Preserve are only open to vehicles in the summer and fall; consequently, not all of these outings may be available at all times of the year.

Wilderness Camping in the Adirondacks

Hiking and paddling in the Adirondack Forest Preserve is great—awesome, actually. I have always appreciated camping as one of the most intimate ways to get to know a place. The additional investment of time (compared to a day trip) allows me to see and hear more, with the freedom to explore more as well. Experiencing the wilderness in the daylight hours is only half of the experience; nighttime brings forth an additional layer of sensory stimulation. Having companions around with whom to share the campfire makes the night all the richer.

That being said, an activity that comes intuitively to some people might be intimidating to others who are curious about the concept of wilderness camping but have never had the opportunity to try it before. Others might be experienced backpackers but are new to the Adirondacks. This book can't be a primer for "how to camp," but I can use these next few pages to address a few common concerns.

Wilderness and Wild Forest

The Adirondack Forest Preserve comprises some 3 million acres of constitutionally protected public lands, maintained in a "forever wild" status. Although forestry is practiced on private lands throughout the park, none is permitted on lands owned by the state; any evidence of logging you may encounter in the preserve will always be historical in nature, dating from before the land was protected. Many of the older state land parcels are therefore graced with forests of exquisite beauty, simply because they have been left undisturbed for all that time.

Although the entire Forest Preserve exists in this near-wilderness state, slightly less than half of it is officially recognized as wilderness—that is, as the 1964 Wilderness Act states, land "where the earth and its community of life are untrammeled by man—where man himself is a visitor who does not remain."

Because this is state land, not a national forest or park, the Wilderness Act does not apply. Instead, New York implements its own wilderness designation to qualifying lands in the Adirondack and Catskill Parks, which in some ways is even more protective than the federal standard. For instance, the minimum threshold in the Adirondacks is 10,000 acres, compared to the 5,000 acres permitted by the Wilderness Act.

Otherwise, the state and federal definitions of wilderness are remarkably similar—and not by coincidence. Howard Zahniser, the author of the Wilderness Act, knew the Adirondacks well and owned a small cabin just outside of what is now the Siamese Ponds Wilderness. He drew inspiration from New York's "forever-wild clause," and when the Adirondack Park Agency designated the first wilderness areas in 1972, the state returned the favor by cribbing heavily from Zahniser's bill.

Today there are twenty designated wilderness areas in Adirondack Park, ranging in size from the 7,896-acre Jay Mountain Wilderness (the only exception to the minimum-size threshold) to the massive 272,000-acre High Peaks Wilderness. Several Adirondack areas outclass the next nearest large wildernesses in New Hampshire and West Virginia by wide margins, offering possibilities for remoteness that would be difficult to recreate in most other eastern states. Protected environments extend from the depths of the Hudson Gorge to the alpine zone on Mount Marcy, with a little bit of everything in between.

The second major Forest Preserve land classification is called "wild forest," which has no close parallel in the federal land management lexicon. The primary difference is that the wild forest designation permits motor vehicles and bicycles, and access roads do tend to penetrate deeper into the backcountry. That said, the empty spaces between the roads are often every much as wild as the protected wilderness areas, thanks to the forever-wild status of the entire Forest Preserve.

The outings described in this book make good use of both designations—with a decided bias toward the wilderness areas, simply because of their spaciousness and their specialty in providing outdoor experiences beyond the reach of motor vehicles. That being said, many of the wild forests include pockets of de facto wilderness and should not be dismissed.

If you would like to learn more about the various wilderness and wild forest areas, I invite you to peruse my descriptions of them at https://adirondackwilderness.org/explore-the-adirondack-wilderness/.

Lean-tos and Designated Campsites

On public land as spacious as the Adirondack Forest Preserve, the camping opportunities are theoretically infinite. State regulations allow at-large camping in many areas, so long as you pick a spot that's at least 150 feet from the nearest road, trail, or source of water. With this in mind, almost any random spot in the forest could potentially be a valid campsite.

But that's not what this book is about. Nor is that how most people camp.

The most attractive campsites are those located in interesting areas. In the Adirondacks this means one located on the shore of a pond or lake, on the banks of a river or stream, or those located at the hub of a mountain trail system. If a sense of solitude can be achieved, all the better. Any good campsite will have a reliable source of water, a source of firewood that hasn't been depleted by frequent use, and something interesting to see or do while you are in the area.

Therefore, this book focuses on established campsites legally sanctioned by the DEC. Such campsites are plentiful, and all the ones described in this guide should be easy to find.

When we speak of "wilderness camping," we are speaking of a primitive form of camping. (If by any chance someone is envisioning indoor plumbing and soft beds, we need to have a talk.) The poshest sites will be distinguished by a picnic table, but even those are exceedingly rare. Most are just a spot of level ground with a simple fireplace. There may or may not be a privy nearby. These are all of the amenities one should expect to find.

Duck Hole No. 1 lean-to. *Photo courtesy of the author*

Lean-tos

Lean-tos are an Adirondack specialty; in fact, other states sometimes refer to their trail shelters as "Adirondack shelters." These are three-sided log structures in various states of maintenance/decay, scattered throughout the Forest Preserve. Inspired by the temporary bark shelters constructed on the fly by nineteenth-century guides, the current models are somewhat more substantial and can withstand the use of decades. Conservation officials began providing log lean-tos in the 1910s, perfected their design soon after, and have been keeping things more or less the same ever since.

Today there are hundreds of lean-tos available to the camping public, and because they are easier to portray on trail maps most novice backpackers have an easier time finding them. Their presence or absence can sometimes affect patterns of usage on entire trail networks, with people gravitating to the ponds that have lean-tos while eschewing those nearby that "only" have tent sites.

Lean-tos are also preferred because they tend to provide a more consistent experience: each provides an elevated floor, a decent roof, a nearby privy, and access to water in one form or another. They are less good at providing privacy, however, since most are intended to be easily found—they are often located directly on trails, which means even passing day hikers will be walking through your site.

These shelters also come with a long tradition of sharing. While technically not a regulation, the idea that a lean-to should be shared up to its capacity is so engrained in the minds of campers it has become a mantra. This can lead to communal encounters among perfect strangers. Socially minded people find this idea attractive, and soloists find it a major turn-off. The "rule" about sharing lean-tos suggests the maximum capacity is eight people, but in my experience that is an ambitious number; floor space can start to become snug with four people (plus their gear), and awkwardly cozy with six vying for elbow room.

Designated Campsites

I have the habit of referring to "designated campsites," "primitive campsites," and "tent sites" in a way that may lead some people to assume these are distinct concepts, but each phrase is jargon for the same thing: a wilderness campsite without a lean-to. These are even more numerous than lean-tos and thus provide a wider array of opportunities and experiences. However, other than the ones sited along canoe routes, their locations are often less well publicized and thus many tend to go unnoticed by the novices.

One of the tricky aspects of dealing with primitive campsites is distinguishing the legal sites from the informal (and sometimes blatantly illegal) sites worn from frequent usage. I have run afoul of this myself by camping at a spot that looked like a campsite and had been used as such for years, but which an unamused assistant forest ranger insisted was not officially recognized by the DEC—just as my companions and I were settling in for a peaceful night in the woods.

In theory (if not always in practice) a legal campsite will be designated with a yellow "camp here" disc—hence the term *designated campsite*. Rather than inadvertently inspiring readers to repeat the same mistake I made, I have tried my best to pick a list of sites where it would be difficult to go wrong. Many campsites are located off-trail and thus appeal to people who value privacy, but the ones I am writing about in this book should be as easy to find as the lean-tos.

Designated campsite marker. *Photo courtesy of the author*

Campsite amenities are sparse, to say the least: they consist only of some level ground for a tent or two, a crude fireplace, and maybe a privy nearby—though often not. My favorite sites are those located near a rock ledge with a scenic view over a remote lake, but there are so many choice campsites located throughout the backcountry that, to be totally honest, I have dozens of favorite sites.

Canoe Camping

Canoe camping can involve both lean-tos and designated campsites. The rules are all the same, but the culture for canoe camping in the Adirondacks is slightly different than the backpacking culture.

For instance, water-access campsites tend to be well mapped and easier to find. On the larger waterbodies, they are numbered with signs visible from the water, and they are scattered all along the shore and islands. Paddlers are instinctively more privacy conscious as well and will avoid sites if it is obvious from a distance they are being used . . . although waterside lean-tos still have a magnetic hold on the minds of many campers.

For the sake of simplicity, I will refer to "canoes" and "canoe camping" throughout the waterway portion of this book, even though kayakers have been known to take umbrage at what they perceive as an implicit bias. As far as I'm concerned, if your preferred watercraft is powered by your arms and stows everything you need for a weekend of camping, then it's all part of the same family.

Enjoying the Outdoors

The Adirondacks are vast, but its wilderness is comparatively benign. People venture out on expeditions of personal importance every week of the year, and it is rare that they end in misfortune. Still, wilderness travel always involves challenge and risk, and that holds true here, too. Things can and do happen, and some people have been known to either underestimate the terrain or overestimate their own capabilities. Careful planning goes a long way.

Biting Flies

Biting flies are almost an inevitability for any wilderness experience in the Adirondacks, at least from May through September. However, there are ways of coping with their presence or even minimizing their impact. There are three primary varieties that everyone complains about, plus two other more specialized pests that are somewhat easier to avoid. The earliest biters hatch in April and the last are not chased away until after Labor Day, with "peak season" occurring from May through early July.

Among the first to appear are the blackflies, better described as gnats than flies. They are distinguished by their tendency to swarm during the height of their season—usually a few weeks bracketing Memorial Day—although they can often be found as early as April and as late as July. They are easily defeated by cool, breezy weather, but warm weather can drive them into a frenzy. Only the hardiest souls eke out a measure of happiness in these conditions.

Mosquitoes are the next most common flying-and-biting pest. They too begin to hatch in April, but they are not likely to become annoying until June and July. Only in extreme conditions do they swarm as much as blackflies.

Deer flies are the largest of the "big three," and the loudest. They are active not only during the hottest days of June and July but also during the hottest hours. Sometimes they are accompanied by a larger (but less common) variety called "moose flies." Deer flies like to burrow into your hair and also find dogs difficult to resist. Humans find some relief simply by wearing a hat.

The other two common (but less universal) biting flies are no-see-ums and stable flies. The former are not really invisible, but they tend not to be noticed until after they've bitten, thus the name. No-see-ums descend at dusk and stick close to water, so you can usually escape them by backing into the woods.

Stable flies look like common house flies but have a stinging bite. They peak around Labor Day (after most other pests have faded for the season), and this can make them a late-summer spoiler. Their alternate name is "ankle biters," which is apt, but they also have a fondness for dogs. They are as impossible to swat as houseflies, but they are usually only encountered over water.

All of these insects are a standard part of any Adirondack experience and can only be completely avoided by avoiding the summer season altogether. In my experience each person has their own comfort threshold, and what is "tolerable" for one camper will be "insane" for the next. Attitude goes a long way, but repellent, long-sleeve clothing, and cool, breezy days also help.

Deer Ticks

Not very many years ago I was agnostic about the threat of ticks penetrating the Adirondacks. Historically these arachnids were not associated with the region and were the last things on anyone's mind. However, ticks did exist in heavy numbers just outside Adirondack Park, and now they are making clear inroads into the wilderness. I no longer doubt their presence; I've had to pick them off me several times while in the backcountry.

Tick numbers are still light in the Forest Preserve, but they are clearly expanding their range. If all we had to worry about were the arachnids themselves, the "ick factor" would be their greatest threat. The modus operandi for ticks is to lie in wait for someone to pass by and then hitch a ride. If successful, the tick will latch onto the victim's skin and remain attached until it becomes engorged—bloated to about the size of a jellybean—and then fall off. The process may take weeks.

They also have several advantages working in their favor, including a small size (about the size of a poppy seed) and an indestructible body. But what makes the presence of ticks worrisome is the host of diseases they can transmit—Lyme disease being just the tip of the iceberg.

Ticks are active at any time the ground is not covered by snow but, in my experience, are most visible in spring and fall. They may be lurking in the brush beside a trail or in the leaf litter on the forest floor. For humans passing through these newly colonized territories, the only defenses are constant bodily awareness and long clothing (which you may choose to treat with permethrin).

If one should attach itself to your skin, remove it as soon as possible—but carefully, to avoid squeezing the contents of its abdomen into your bloodstream. If a bull's-eye rash develops around the bite, or should you experience any illness, you will need to seek medical care.

Dogs should be pretreated with tick repellents prior to your camping trip.

Bears, Rodents, and Other Campsite Invaders

Black bears are the largest omnivores in the Adirondacks, other than *Homo sapiens*. They have developed a reputation for raiding campsites in search of backpackers' food, especially in the ever-popular High Peaks Wilderness—though bear encounters have been recorded in all parts of Adirondack Park.

The average black bear is not a threat to campers. They are smart creatures, however, and inevitably some will figure out that backpacks contain food. Unfortunately, those who become nuisances are not able to unlearn this behavior, and the result is often a death sentence for the bear. Importantly, though, these bears could never have learned to associate people with the food they carry if the people visiting their habitat took better care of their food.

It is not inevitable that a bear will raid your campsite; if you find yourself having multiple encounters, please consider that you are doing something horrifically wrong (or repeatedly visiting areas with high levels of both bear and human traffic). Managing your food is largely a matter of managing your food odors. If your meals (or their empty wrappers) are not adequately contained, you may be broadcasting your presence to the local wildlife.

The traditional method for safeguarding food at a wilderness campsite has long been to hang a waterproof "bear bag" from a tree in such a way that bears (and other critters) cannot reach it from the ground or from the tree itself. This works if done properly, but it's far from foolproof—just check out the snagged and abandoned rope adorning many a tree. Instead, the only method known to work in nearly all situations is to store all of your food and hygiene products in a bear canister, a small keg made out of hard plastic that a bear may bat around but theoretically can't pry open.

More numerous than bears, though, are the rodents—which have caused me more grief than any bear ever has. Again, the issue will be poorly contained food odors. But rather than mugging you in broad daylight like a black bear might do, mice will chew their way through any material in their way—including backpacks and tent walls—to get what they want. That's assuming they can smell where you've stowed your food and know ahead of time where to chew.

Camping with Dogs

Outside the High Peaks Wilderness and certain other facilities, there are no leash requirements in the Adirondack Forest Preserve. Therefore, this is a haven for dogs who crave an outdoor experience unlike anything possible in some fenced-in municipal park. Dogs love to hike and camp as much as people do! A few are even pros at riding calmly in canoes. That being said, not all canines have the chops to be "adventure dogs," and the wilderness is not completely without risk for them.

Every dog is an individual, and not all of them have the temperament to leave wildlife alone, or to resist the urge to run. It's important, then, to always carry a leash, even if it's not a requirement to use it. If you are unsure how your dog will react to the freedom of the woods, then begin conservatively.

There is plenty of wildlife in the woods, and all dogs will be stimulated by the scents they encounter. But of all the wild denizens they might find, the most troubling will be porcupines—slow-moving creatures that many dogs can't resist investigating, much to their peril. Removing quills from a dog's face is neither easy nor painless—it's best to abandon your camping trip and go seek a veterinarian's services. Speaking from experience, some dogs learn slowly from their misadventures.

A collapsible water bowl is useful to help keep dogs hydrated on hot, dry days. There are a variety of dog backpacks available on the market, but despite their quality, not all dogs may take to them. And don't be surprised when your dog decides on a whim to go swimming—with the backpack still on and a weekend's worth of kibble still inside.

Finally—and it grieves me that this needs to be put into words—if you choose to bag your dog's droppings, fine, but take the bag with you. There are no maids in the wilderness other than your own two hands. Strictly speaking, "poop bags" aren't even necessary; the woods are big,

Paddling Henderson Lake. *Photo courtesy of the author*

and this isn't suburbia. Kicking the droppings out of the footpath is a perfectly acceptable solution—and it's already more than the wild coyotes do.

Safe and Responsible Wilderness Recreation

The backcountry is a rugged area where cell phone coverage is apt to be limited and help may not be just a phone call away. A little bit of preparation therefore goes a long way. The following are some basic tips that are easy to follow and will better your chances of having a safe and enjoyable journey.

Always let someone know where you are going. Provide your hiking itinerary and your expected return time to someone reliable—and particularly someone who will notice if you don't make it home. In the event you are overdue from a camping adventure, that person should be prepared to call either 911 or the Forest Ranger Dispatch at 833-NYS-RANGERS (833-697-7264).

Carry a map and compass. This may sound old school, but it works. Mindlessly following a trail is a fine strategy until you miss a turn and have to troubleshoot where you went wrong. Maps and compasses require no battery and will not die on you. By investing the personal effort to know and understand your route, it is easier to determine your location and get back to where you want to be.

Always carry water with you, or bring along the means to purify water from streams and lakes. The presence of giardia makes most backcountry water sources suspect.

Keep your group sizes small. There is no overarching regulation for the entire Adirondack Park governing overnight group sizes, but the most advisable cap is eight people—and practically speaking, even that is somewhat large. Yes, the woods may be big, but campsites (even lean-tos) tend to be small; prime real estate (i.e., level, dry ground located comfortably far from the fireplace and privy) often disappears fast on a group camping trip. Remember, all tents should be set up within 15 feet of the designated campsite marker.

For canoeing, state regulations require that one personal flotation device (PFD) be kept on board for each passenger. Children under twelve years of age are required to wear a PFD at all times, as are adults between November 1 and May 1.

Never wear cotton clothing, including denim. Once it gets wet, cotton is very slow to dry, and once the weather turns cold nothing will sap your energy like the sensation of being dressed in a wet washcloth.

In addition to your camping gear, always carry insect repellent, sunscreen, lip balm, matches, a headlamp, a first aid kit, extra snacks, a knife, a whistle, a rain jacket, and a wool sweater, even in summer. Conditions can change quickly in the mountains, so adaptability pays dividends.

When camping, be sure to use only established sites and build a campfire using only dead and down wood. Green wood doesn't burn, and no one wants to look at the stumps years later. Much of the top layer of soil in an Adirondack forest is duff, which is made of decomposed plant matter. Duff is combustible, and once it is ignited by a poorly located campfire it may smolder for days, leaving a large pit in the campsite and killing the roots of any trees in its path. There is one really good way to prevent a duff fire, and that is to thoroughly douse your campfire before you leave.

Practice low-impact hiking and camping techniques, meaning that the next person to come along shouldn't have to clean up after you or count the many ways you left your mark. You came in search of a fresh, unblemished landscape, so allow others to have that pleasure, too. Visit Leave No Trace at https://lnt.org for more information.

If you are unsure of your abilities in the wilderness, then join a group! Here in the internet age there is no shortage of ways to seek out hiking clubs and meetup groups that suit your interest.

PART I

LEAN-TOS

For many people, the Adirondack lean-to is as much an icon of the wilderness as a loon, a moose, or a tall pine tree. These trail shelters evolved over the course of several decades, from the traditional rustic designs that nineteenth-century guides once improvised on the spot from materials found onsite, to the standard design of peeled logs and dimensional lumber now used by the Department of Environmental Conservation. Much of that evolution occurred prior to World War I, but the design has only been perfected ever since.

Many people prefer lean-tos for the lore that surrounds them and because they are often the most convenient campsites available in the backcountry. By "convenient" I mean they provide a roof, three walls, and a floor—as well as a privy of some kind in the nearby woods.

If you have never camped in a lean-to, you will probably become hooked your first time out. They are available on a first-come basis and provide comfortable sleeping space for four people; six people can usually fit somewhat snugly, but eight starts to become crowded. Although all are very similar in design, each has its own character in setting. Some face directly toward a scenic vista; others take advantage of a nearby rock to reflect heat back inside. Most come equipped with logbooks to let you record your stay, and to read about the experiences of those who came before you.

The advantages of a lean-to are obvious when it rains, but less so when the bugs are out in force. If you are camping at a lean-to site, the regulatory preference is that you actually *use* the lean-to. Although it is a common practice, setting tents up either inside or around the lean-to is discouraged—even though this provides better protection from the bugs.

Cedar Lakes No. 1 lean-to. *Photo courtesy of the author*

One common feature of most lean-tos is their relative popularity, with the resulting side effect that firewood can be scarce in the immediate vicinity. If you are able to gather more than you need, store the extra supply inside the shelter where it will remain dry for the next person who comes along.

1 Bear Lake

Synopsis: A short hike to a secluded pond in a serene setting
Hiking Distance: 1.4 miles (summer)
Elevation Change: 435 feet

There are many lakes and ponds in the Adirondacks named "Bear," but this one near the hamlet of McKeever has always been one of my favorites. It is found at the end of a short hike, located in an area of the southwestern Adirondacks known for its many easy-to-reach destinations. But of all the hikes in this particular area, I have long gravitated toward Bear because its trails are designated expressly for hiking—and therefore have a more natural appearance—in a setting that is perfectly serene.

The lean-to at Bear Lake is a relative newcomer, built of cedar logs in 2010 by a volunteer group known as Lean2Rescue. The structure is set back from the small lake and does not face the water, but the construction is superb and has possibly one of the highest ceilings you will find in an Adirondack lean-to. The old tent sites nearer the water still exist, although most people now prefer the shelter.

The trail to Bear Lake is not far from the busy NY 28 highway corridor, the principal thoroughfare to Old Forge. However, the trailhead is tucked away on a little side road leading into state land, which is only open seasonally—late May through the end of hunting season.

When the seasonal Wolf Lake Landing Road is open, this hike is a mere 1.4 miles long. Bear Lake would be a worthwhile destination in any season but is best in summer and fall, when backpackers can take advantage of the shorter trail miles and therefore make a quick getaway into the woods.

Getting There

Near the south end of the Moose River bridge on NY 28 between Old Forge and Otter Lake, turn east onto McKeever Road. Where this road curves left, bear right on a driveway that passes near a former

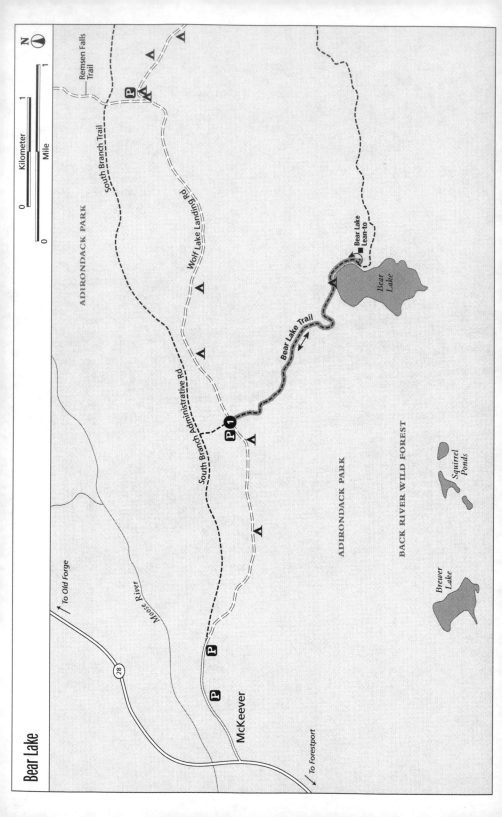

railroad station, following the signs that promise access to state land. Cross the Adirondack Scenic Railroad tracks and follow the driveway into the woods, coming to a pair of large parking areas about 0.7 miles from the state highway.

Wolf Lake Landing Road (a narrow gravel road suitable for most cars in normal conditions) veers right from this first parking area. When the gate is open, you can drive an additional 1.2 miles to a marked intersection with the blue-marked foot trail to Bear Lake. The small parking area is crude in design and holds no more than two or three cars.

The Trail

The blue-marked foot trail leads southeast from Wolf Lake Landing Road, cutting through a low-lying wet area before beginning to climb. A sharp left turn leads into a long draw, through which you climb 185 feet to a height-of-land at 0.6 miles. You are now standing on the ridge that enfolds the north end of Bear Lake, and the 250-foot descent that follows is one of the highlights of the trip, leading you below an impressive rock wall—at least, impressive for this gentle corner of the Adirondacks. If it has rained recently, there may be a trickle of water spilling down its face.

You reach the north shore where there is a small sandy beach—always a pleasant place to stop, where you can get your feet wet and enjoy the view down the length of the lake. At first glance this looks like it would be a good swimming spot, too. The bottom of the lake is mucky, however, and if you stir the sediment up too much you are sure to rouse the attention of a leech or two.

The trail continues around the east side, where at 1.4 miles a side trail leads left to the lean-to, one of the most structurally aesthetic and well-built shelters you will find anywhere on state land. The only complaint some visitors may have is that it does not face the water, although the shoreline is just a short stroll away.

Beyond the lean-to spur, the main trail quickly reaches a sizeable inlet stream that you will need to hop across. There is an intersection on the other side with a yellow-marked trail that leads to Bloodsucker Pond and Woodhull Lake. The main blue-marked trail continues south

Bear Lake lean-to. *Photo courtesy of the author*

along the shoreline before pulling away to the southeast, ultimately connecting with the multiuse trail system near Bear Creek Road to the south. However, this trail junction near the inlet stream is as far as many hikers choose to go.

2　Queer Lake

Synopsis: A classic hike through an old-growth forest to a popular lean-to
Hiking Distance: 3.4 miles
Elevation Change: Rolling terrain

Queer Lake gets its name from its unusual shape, divided nearly into three separate bodies of water by prominent peninsulas. It is a popular destination, but public use is focused almost exclusively at two points along the shoreline: one at the tip of the northern bay, where trails first approach Queer Lake, and the other at the lean-to perched at the base of the northern peninsula.

The lake sits in the southern half of the Pigeon Lake Wilderness, an area nearly 50,000 acres in size that for the most part was never logged. This wilderness is named (indirectly) for the extinct passenger pigeon, great flocks of which were known to roost in the area. Perhaps the results of a destabilized ecological system, passenger pigeon populations exploded at some point after the European colonization of North America, their flocks numbering in the thousands—if not *billions*—throughout the seventeenth and eighteenth centuries. An abundance of beech nuts would have attracted them to the area surrounding the remote wilderness lake that now bears their name—at least until their numbers fatally plummeted by the end of the nineteenth century. The last passenger pigeon died in captivity in 1914.

Most modern visitors probably pass through these woods unaware of the absence. Rather, this hike is today known for the way it offers a sense of the primeval in a reasonably accessible area, not far from popular vacation destinations. The hike is not *all* pristine and untouched—the trail makes a strategic detour around a private inholding—but it does pass for an otherwise excellent hike.

Getting There

Follow NY 28 to the hamlet of Eagle Bay, located near the Herkimer-Hamilton county line at Fourth Lake. From there, Big Moose Road

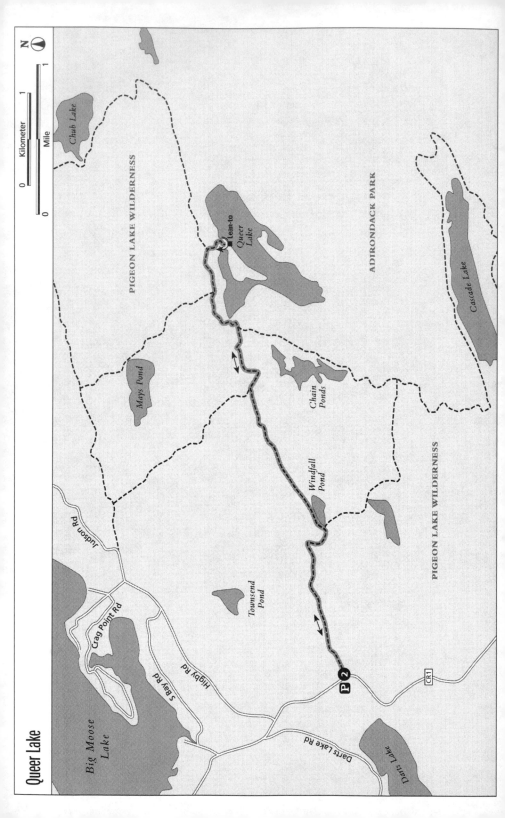

Queer Lake

leads northwest out of town and into state land. There are multiple trail-head parking areas (some will be revisited elsewhere in this guidebook), but for this recommended hike, stop at the Windfall Pond Trailhead on the right side of the road, 3.3 miles from Eagle Bay.

The Trail

This is a multiphased hike passing various streams and waterbodies—and no fewer than five trail junctions—en route to the lean-to at Queer Lake. The route is hilly in both directions, but its highly visible trailhead and attractive destination makes it a well-used trail throughout the year.

From the trailhead on Big Moose Road, the trail ventures east-ward into the woods and makes the first stream crossing within a few minutes, then again a few minutes later. These first two crossings are assisted by substantial bridges, but after passing a wetland your next set of crossings will all be hop-a-rock affairs. Generally the stream is never big enough to be an obstacle.

At 1.1 miles you reach a trail junction at the outlet of Windfall Pond. Bear left and cross the stream one last time, and then circle the north shore of the pond. At about 1.2 miles (roughly 0.1 miles after the last ford), a path leads right to a lightly used campsite on Windfall, perhaps the best place on this pond to stop for views. Otherwise the trail hurries past the pond, heading northeast as it contours along the side of a hill.

At 2.1 miles you reach the second trail junction. This time bear right, following the trail to Queer Lake as it climbs abruptly up the same hill it has so far been seeming to avoid. Soon after reaching the top it drops back down to its prior elevation. The purpose for this ver-tical detour is a private cabin tucked away in the woods, perhaps just far enough off the trail not to be seen, accessed from the area around Big Moose Lake. Immediately upon reaching the foot of the hill and crossing a small stream, the public trail bears right and makes the final approach to Queer Lake.

Your first glimpse comes at 2.6 miles, where you reach the third trail intersection. An unmarked path continues straight to a spot known locally as Queer Lake Landing. However, this is just the northern bay,

Queer Lake lean-to. *Photo courtesy of the author*

and the lean-to is directly opposite this view. To get there you will need to bear left at the trail signs and climb once more into the hills, passing the side trails to Mays Pond (3 miles from the trailhead) and Chub Lake (at 3.2 miles) before descending again to water level. Here you cross a narrow isthmus onto the northern peninsula, and after crossing a sharp little knoll you reach the lean-to from behind, 3.4 miles from Big Moose Road.

This route is only one of several approaches to Queer Lake, so don't be surprised to find people already here even if you've seen no one on the trail all day. That said, the lean-to's popularity has never seemed overwhelming. It sits in an attractive spot partly shielded by brush, but with paths leading down to the water (including one miniature sand "beach" that suggests a cold swim).

Also, don't be surprised if firewood is in scarce supply. My one gripe about the Queer Lake lean-to has long been the "stump forest" that surrounds it—incriminating evidence left by boneheaded campers who mistakenly believed cutting live trees was legal and provided viable firewood. They were wrong on both counts. These stumps have been moldering away for decades, and there is no need to contribute to their number. If you need to find wood, follow the trail back toward Big Moose—serving your own needs but also helping to clear the trail in the process.

3 Gulf Brook and Biesemeyer Lean-tos

Synopsis: A relatively short and easy hike to a pair of popular lean-tos with nearby climbing options

Hiking Distance: 1.1 miles to Gulf Brook lean-to; 2.1 miles to Biesemeyer lean-to

Vertical Rise: Relatively level to Gulf Brook; 450-foot vertical rise to Lost Pond

State officials designated the Hurricane Mountain Wilderness in 2010 from a former "primitive area" of the same name. At 14,222 acres, this is one of the more compact protected areas in the Adirondacks, and nearly all of it consists of mid- to high-elevation slopes, protecting the montane region but almost none of the lower elevations. A significant chunk of the climbing is done in your car on the drive to the trailhead. Thus, in this one area, hikers can reach the higher elevations without the usual effort required to reach it.

Unlike the other mountainous wilderness areas in Adirondack Park, this one is hemmed in by residential zones on several sides, making it more stereotypical of wilderness areas in the eastern United States. (One wonders about possible barriers to wildlife, which would otherwise be passing in and out of the wilderness boundaries.) These observations aside, however, the northernmost trailhead in the Hurricane Mountain Wilderness—called Crow Clearing—is the hub of an interesting hiking network. Located high above the hamlet of Keene, this one starting point boasts the possibility of several distinct adventures: the short climb to Big Crow Mountain (2,815 feet), the more rugged climb to Weston Mountain (3,183 feet), and the classic climb to Hurricane Mountain itself (3,678 feet).

At the center of this network, more or less, is a pair of lean-tos spaced roughly a mile apart from each other. Neither shelter is particularly scenic, but their location makes them integral to any of the mountain adventures this place is best known for. To be sure, one really doesn't need to camp out to enjoy any of these climbs, but both shelters provide a tempting taste of the Adirondacks' higher elevations.

Gulf Brook and Biesemeyer Lean-tos

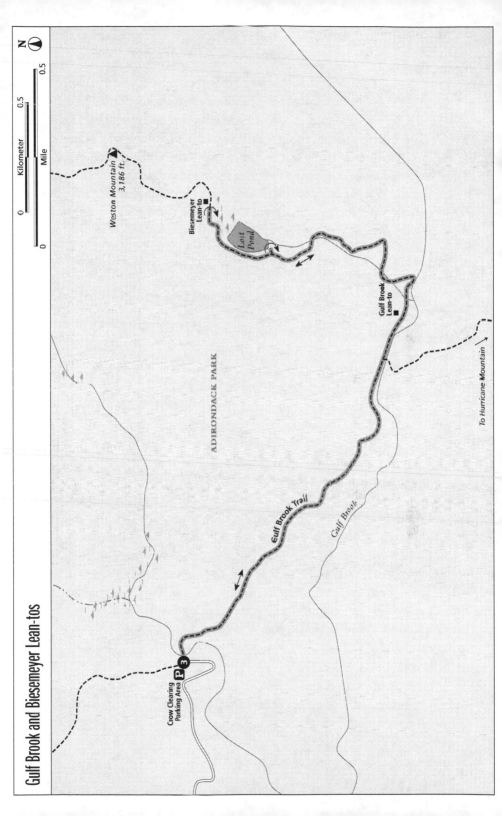

Getting There

You can find the Crow Clearing Trailhead by following NY 73 to downtown Keene, where Hurricane Road heads east, beginning next to the town offices. Follow Hurricane Road uphill for 2.2 miles, where O'Toole Lane bears left. This is a winding gravel road that continues to climb into the mountains. At 3 miles you reach the end of winter plowing, and here the road narrows even further. The parking area, 3.3 miles from Keene, was actually once the site of someone's house. The modern parking area—rustic as it is—forms a circle around the old cellar hole.

The Trail

Of the two trails radiating outward from Crow Clearing, you want the one that leads east, with signs promising destinations at Hurricane Mountain, Gulf Brook, and Lost Pond. The trail crosses a small brook and then proceeds into the woods by following the bed of an abandoned road. If there is any climbing between here and Gulf Brook, it is hardly noticeable; you've already parked your car just a touch over 2,200 feet in elevation; therefore, much of the vertical rise was already accomplished before your boots even hit the ground.

The old road makes a gentle entry into the Gulf Brook valley, and the stream slowly becomes more audible as this first mile progresses. The surrounding forest is emblematic of this part of the Adirondacks, as well as this elevation range: lots of poplar trees (also called aspen) signifying the extent of the forest fires that once swept through here, but also plenty of red spruce and balsam fir, two stalwarts of the montane forest. Sugar maples seem poised to gain in prominence as the forest matures, and birches come in both the paper ("white") and yellow varieties.

After a brisk mile of hiking, you reach a junction. Most people bear right, across Gulf Brook, on the northern trail to Hurricane Mountain's summit. The old roadbed keeps left. A small clearing between the two forks was the site of the old Gulf Brook lean-to, now closed to camping as it gradually revegetates.

To find the new Gulf Brook lean-to, stay on the old roadbed for an additional 0.1 miles. The shelter stands to the left on the hill above the

Gulf Brook lean-to. *Photo courtesy of the author*

trail, beside a small stream. The woods are open, with plenty of shady hardwoods but very little undergrowth. Were it not for the lean-to, this slope would hardly recommend itself for camping.

Lost Pond. *Photo courtesy of the author*

The second lean-to is another mile deeper into the mountains. To find it, return to the old roadbed—still an excellent hiking trail—and continue east. The road itself comes to an abrupt end at 1.2 miles, but the hiking trail continues without missing a beat. It bears left and begins a long, gentle climb, rising about 400 feet to the outlet of Lost Pond, which you reach at 1.8 miles.

The beavers didn't make Lost Pond to please people; the shoreline is wet and marshy, and you have to pick your approaches carefully if you want to enjoy the view. But they certainly picked an excellent location! Lost Pond is not so much "lost" as it is tucked away on a mountainous shelf. Such views as can be found tend to be quite good, with rocky ridges to the north (Weston Mountain among them) and the unmistakable cone of Hurricane Mountain to the south, capped by its fire tower.

As you continue following the trail, Lost Pond devolves into inaccessible marshes. The second lean-to sits in the woods just beyond these marshes, 2.1 miles from Crow Clearing. Known as the Biesemeyer lean-to in honor of a German immigrant who once operated the Mountain

House in Keene with his wife, this is actually among the higher shelters in the Adirondacks. The climate is cool, the surrounding woods are thick, and despite the presence of Lost Pond potable water is not always easily found without walking some distance.

Official trail markers end here, but not the trail itself. The well-worn route continues another 0.4 miles to the summit of Weston Mountain, roughly 300 feet above Lost Pond.

4 Raquette Falls

Synopsis: An undulating hike along a little-used horse trail, providing access to multiple lean-tos on the Raquette River
Hiking Distance: 4.3 miles, with various other lean-tos at odd intervals
Elevation Change: Relatively level

This underappreciated hike along the Raquette River passes no fewer than five lean-tos, including one just 0.2 miles from the trailhead and another unassuming shelter within spitting distance of a ranger station. If you are dead set on camping in a lean-to on your next adventure, few hiking routes are this well endowed with options.

The flipside is that all but one of these shelters stand on the banks of the Raquette River, making them equally accessible to boats and canoes. This puts backpackers in direct competition with paddlers for the best spots, and on busy weekends, the paddlers (and boaters) may have the advantage.

While the trail may not be the most visually exciting wilderness route—and the ranch-like ranger station at the falls may break the wilderness spell—it nevertheless deserves more attention than it seems to get. People seeking the scenic charms of Raquette Falls are more apt to approach in canoes or motorboats, but this same trail in any other part of Adirondack Park would be highly regarded as a recreational asset. Here, it suffers only by comparison.

Between Long Lake and Tupper Lake, the Raquette River is mostly wide and tranquil. Although it forms a portion of the western boundary for the High Peaks Wilderness, the river itself is not part of the wilderness and thus motorboats are permitted. However, a mile-long section in the middle of this stretch is unnavigable, culminating with the thunderous plunge at "Lower" Raquette Falls.

None of the five lean-tos are located within view of the falls, although the last two are close enough for a quick stroll whenever the mood strikes. Several designated campsites are also sprinkled between these two shelters.

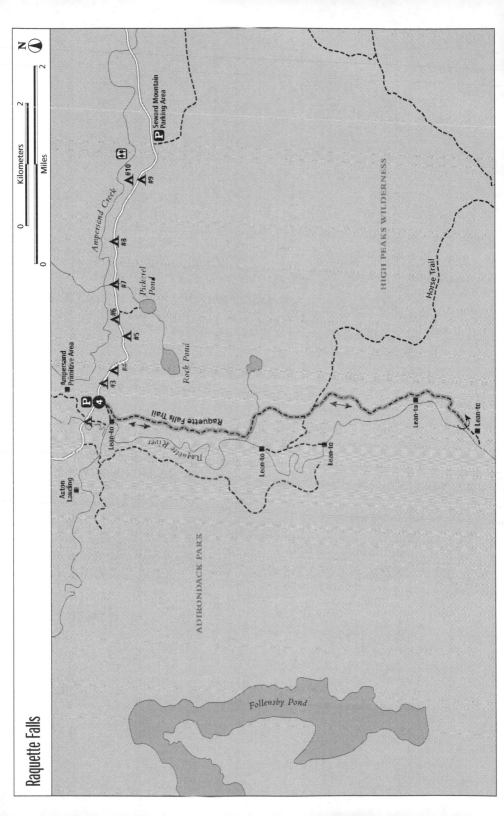

Raquette Falls

Getting There

The trailhead is located on Coreys Road, which begins on NY 3 about 2.6 miles east of the junction with NY 30, between the villages of Tupper Lake and Saranac Lake. This begins as a residential road but quickly becomes a gravel lane leading almost entirely through state land—much of it a reforestation area of pines. The trailhead parking area is on the right at 2.7 miles, just after the bridge over Stony Creek.

The Trail

The trail to Raquette Falls is an abandoned road that was later designated for horse use, although to my knowledge it is no longer frequently used by horses. But this history explains the route's easiness, with gentle grades and wide turns.

The first thing that happens as you leave the trailhead is the fork to the right, which leads to the Stony Creek lean-to just 0.2 miles from the parking area. (Despite its name, it stands on the Raquette River and is therefore accessible to boats and canoes. Across the Raquette is a forest of gracefully curving silver maples.)

The main trail keeps left for Raquette Falls. The walking conditions are excellent as the horse trail undulates through a forest of mostly hardwoods, with a few hemlock groves and spruce-fir pockets thrown in for good measure. The lowlands surrounding the river are on your right, forming a labyrinth of swamps, pools, and oxbows. Topographically it is a confusing world out there, so be glad to have the clarity of the trail.

At 2.2 miles, a 0.6-mile-long side trail branches off to the right, leading to the Hemlock Hill lean-to out on the river. (Not advertised on official trail signs is the unmarked spur branching south to the Palmer Brook lean-to, 0.7 miles distant.)

The horse trail passes the junction to Calkins Brook at 2.4 miles and then reaches a scenic wetland on Palmer Brook with glimpses of Seward and Donaldson Mountains, two of the westernmost High Peaks. Seward Mountain was named for William Seward, a former New York State governor best known for serving as the U.S. secretary of state under Abraham Lincoln and negotiating the purchase of Alaska.

Raquette Falls. *Photo courtesy of the author*

The trail crosses a small hill and passes close to one of the river's small peripheral ponds. It then cuts a corner through a bay, arriving at roughly 3.6 miles at a fourth lean-to, easily accessible from the trail and designated the Raquette Falls No. 2 lean-to. It is a nice, attractive spot with a good view across the river, a small pond beyond, and a small mountain on the horizon.

Beyond this point, the trail climbs and descends another small hill, with a side path leading to the large pool at the foot of the rapids you have been hearing for some time. After this, at 4.3 miles, you reach the sprawling campus of the Raquette Falls ranger station, which is only staffed by the Department of Environmental Conservation for part of the year. This rustic structure, with its barnlike storage building and nearby field, is like a scene from a western ranch.

There are numerous signs here, for in the summer this is a busy place. One points to a side trail leading 0.2 miles to Lower Falls, one of the three drops comprising Raquette Falls, and easily the most photogenic.

The cascading river is an awesome sight when the water is high—a thunderous, raw, menacing force, like a lion trapped in a cage. This is a massive river.

The main trail continues past the ranger station to a solitary lean-to on the edge of the meadow—the last and loneliest of the five shelters, named Raquette Falls No. 1. It stands beside the trail but far from water. That being said, it is not a horrible site and may be the most dependable for hikers, since this is the only shelter that boats can't reach.

Although this is the most distant lean-to on this hike, it is not necessarily the end of the adventure. Among the reasons I recommend this hike is so backpackers can take advantage of the hiking options here. The obvious is Raquette Falls itself, but the rugged footpath that hugs the east bank of the river provides access to the other cascades comprising Upper and Middle Falls. There is the canoe carry trail leading 0.8 miles upstream from the lean-to to the top of the rapids, as well as the charming footpath leading in about equal distance to secluded Dawson Pond.

5 Duck Hole

Synopsis: A rugged hike to one of the remotest locations in New York
Hiking Distance: 7 miles
Elevation Change: 1,000 feet

The word *hole* in this sense is used to invoke a large valley amid the mountains, akin to its usage in the name of Wyoming's Jackson Hole. Old maps show the original Duck Hole as a small pear-shaped pond located at the confluence of three mountain streams, its outlet uniting these waters to form the Cold River. One imagines it was a favorite haunt of migrating waterfowl.

The period bookended by the years 1912 and 2011 witnessed several significant but widely spaced changes at Duck Hole. This century opened when the Santa Clara Lumber Company—one of several major early landowners in what later became the High Peaks Wilderness—constructed the first dam here, presumably to assist the floating of logs down the Cold River.

More than twenty years later, in 1934–1935, the Civilian Conservation Corps (CCC) constructed a second, more substantial log dam on what was by then state property. This dam stabilized the enlarged pond and was intended as a permanent structure. When the work was done, the CCC crew flung some of their heavy tools into the water.

In later decades the state's Conservation Department (forerunner to today's Department of Environmental Conservation [DEC]) opened an administrative "truck trail" to Duck Hole and constructed a ranger station north of the dam. Although closed to public vehicle access, the road was used frequently by state employees—and not always for official purposes. As the station was equipped with hot and cold water, as well as a stove and refrigerator, off-duty officials would drive in with family members for a weekend of hunting and fishing. Hikers making the trek from Upper Works might encounter several cars parked in the driveway.

After 1972 when this region became the High Peaks Wilderness, the road was closed to all motor vehicles, and the cabin was removed. Horse

Duck Hole

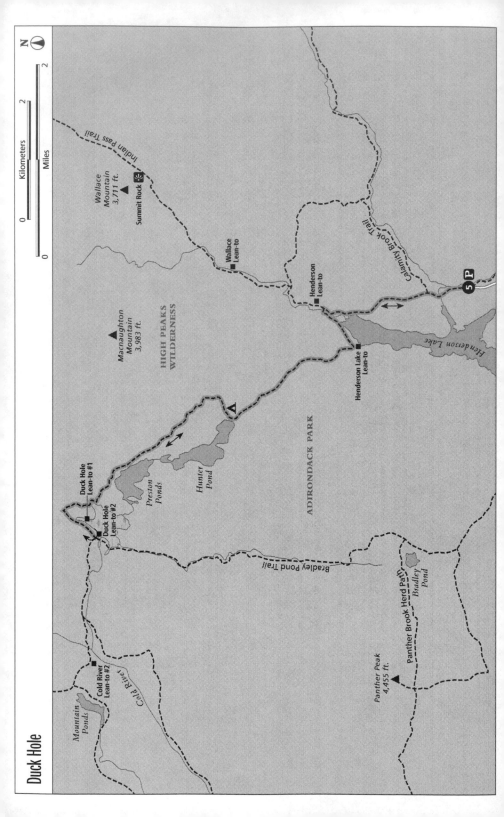

use boomed for a while but declined after a local dude ranch went out of business. The dam and its two attendant lean-tos aged, and a grassy meadow once used for horse grazing filled with brush and flowering weeds.

The century came to an abrupt end in August 2011 when the remnants of Hurricane Irene dumped heavy rains throughout the High Peaks. The torrent of water exploited a weakness at the north end of the CCC dam and washed out a great chunk of the gravel bank, nearly taking the older of the two lean-tos with it. Within days Duck Hole was drained, all but the footprint of the original pond.

Although change continues to transform Duck Hole today, it is now more of the restorative kind, and because of the wilderness designation the DEC has chosen not to interfere. The old lean-to located near the edge of the eroded gulf was removed and replaced with a new structure a short distance away, but nothing has been done to the remains of the dam. The old lake bed had accumulated a deep layer of silt deposits, which were as dangerous as quicksand in autumn 2011 but quickly became a garden of regrowth. Someday a forest of cedar may reclaim these flats, just as their ancestors did in the ancient past.

Today Duck Hole is known as one of the remotest places in the Adirondacks. The loss of the dam provoked a variety of emotional responses in 2011, but in my opinion the event serves as a reminder that some forces of nature cannot be harnessed and controlled. Duck Hole is beginning a new century of recovery and regrowth, and I feel fortunate that I will be able to witness it.

Getting There

From Northway (Interstate 87) Exit 29, drive west on Blue Ridge Road (also called Boreas Road) for 17 miles to the right turn for Tahawus. Follow this road, CR 25, to a fork at 6.3 miles. Turn left and continue to a series of three parking areas: Santanoni at 8.2 miles, East River at 9.2 miles, and the Upper Works parking area at the end of the road, 9.5 miles from Blue Ridge Road. The hike to Duck Hole begins at Upper Works at the end of the road. The parking area is surrounded by a historical site with many interpretive signs; one of the surviving buildings once housed a vacationing Theodore Roosevelt, just days before he became president.

The Trail

From the parking area at the end of the road at Upper Works, pass through the historic site and follow the first 1.8 miles of the trail to Indian Pass. Turn left across the bridge over Indian Pass Brook and follow the trail back south toward the northwest corner of Henderson Lake, reaching a lean-to on the left at 2.4 miles. This shelter was constructed circa 2003 out of precut lumber rather than logs; nearby are the shoreline and an attractive waterfall nestled within a sheltered cove.

The trail now angles generally northwest to follow an unnamed brook. A number of walkways and bridges carry you over the stream, its tributaries, and several wet areas. The climb toward the Preston Ponds is long but relatively gentle. Chains of decrepit wooden walkways lead you into the pass, with mountains rising steeply from it. Preston Ponds Pass is encased in cliffs from which slabs have fallen and lie jagged in the ferns of the wet meadow.

The trail turns right at 4 miles just before the southern shore of Upper Preston Pond. A spur leads to the water and its views to the northwest. Prior to 2003, there was no public access to the pond. Now this is all state-owned Forest Preserve, so linger and enjoy the view all you want. Upper and Lower Preston ponds are both naturally occurring bodies of water, with no vulnerable man-made dams. They are here to stay.

The trail, however, angles away from the pond as soon as it reaches it. It follows a little stream—in it, beside it, and then across it—before angling north to Hunter Pond at 4.3 miles. Just north of the pond, the trail scrambles up a knoll. The climb is short, but it is the steepest hill on the way to Duck Hole.

A long, gentle, sometimes wet descent follows. At 5 miles you reach a tiny opening that was once an old logging clearing, and then you come down to a much larger stream flowing from high up on Mac-Naughton. You immediately cross it without the benefit of a bridge and continue the gentle descent.

Duck Hole. *Photo courtesy of the author*

The trail follows the bank of the stream toward Lower Preston Pond, but you will only glimpse the pond through the trees. Watch for rough and wet conditions at 5.7 miles, where the trail reaches another tributary flowing off of MacNaughton. The terrain is so low that swampy conditions prevail.

The trail climbs and descends two small knolls on the way to Duck Hole, reaching what used to be a log-filled, narrow bay at 6.2 miles. At 6.5 miles you reach Roaring Brook, spanned by a footbridge. The intersection with the Northville-Placid Trail (NPT) is on the far bank.

Turn left on the blue trail. Just past the intersection, the trail is close to another drained finger of Duck Hole, over which there is a view toward Panther Mountain. At 6.8 miles you reach the site of the relocated Duck Hole No. 1 lean-to, built as a new structure just a few years after Hurricane Irene. It sits below the trail on a wooded slope, with a placid stretch of Roaring Brook winding below through the greening lake bed.

The NPT continues southwest for another 0.2 miles to a large clearing, 7 miles from Upper Works. Here there is another intersection, with the N–PT heading right, northwest, from the field and past the site of the old ranger cabin.

The Duck Hole No. 2 lean-to stands to the left, at the edge of the overgrown grazing pasture. The exposed lake bottom has revealed several insights about the construction of the dams. Some of the tools they used were tossed into the lake, and the metal parts were later found in the outlet channel. Elsewhere, parts of the lake bed are dotted with preserved stumps from the original forest, revealing that an extensive cedar grove once stood here. The remaining pond, with only about 20 percent of the surface area of the former reservoir, lies at the southeast end near the outlet of Lower Preston Pond. You can walk freely through much of the former lake bed; however, be suspicious of the exposed silt, which in some places may still be soft enough and wet enough to swallow your boots.

6 Hour Pond

Synopsis: Hike from lake to lake and camp in a basin surrounded by mountains
Hiking Distance: 3.5 miles
Elevation Change: 850 feet

Of the few theories I've heard to explain how this large pond at the foot of Bullhead Mountain got its name, one states it was because Hour Pond was only an hour's hike from Old Farm Clearing, a historic site located south of Thirteenth Lake in what is now the Siamese Ponds Wilderness. Today Old Farm is a plantation of towering Norway spruce trees surrounding a few hidden stone foundations, but in the early twentieth century it was the site of the Thirteenth Lake House, a lodge catering to sportsmen. Prior to that, it was indeed a farm that likely provisioned food to the lumber camps operating throughout Township 13 on the East Branch Sacandaga River. And centuries ago the clearing might've been the sight of an Indian occupation, as hinted by early maps of Warren County.

It is still possible (and enjoyable) to hike to Hour Pond via Old Farm Clearing, but a more exciting route begins at the north end of Thirteenth Lake and cuts southwest through the foothills to intercept the original path. A lean-to located near the east shore of Hour Pond provides a good base for a weekend of exploration. The pond remains a favorite because of its isolated setting, rimmed on three sides by mountains, and the hike from Thirteenth Lake is among the most scenic in the region.

I have my own theory about the pond's name, though. As one passes a summer evening on the shoreline, the sun sets somewhere directly behind the long ridgeline of Bullhead Mountain—roughly an hour ahead of schedule. Do you suppose that's a coincidence?

Getting There

Access to this part of the Siamese Ponds Wilderness—which has much to offer in addition to this hike to Hour Pond—begins on Thirteenth

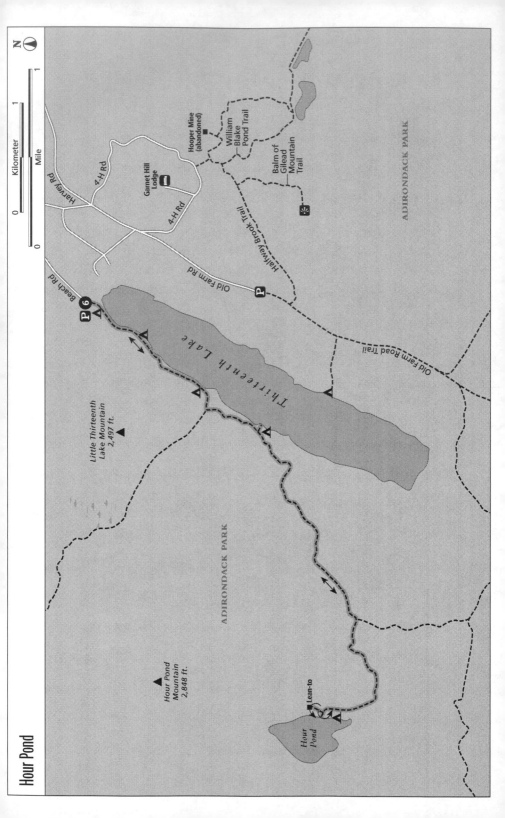

Hour Pond

Lake Road. This paved byway starts on NY 28 in North River and traces a winding course through Christian Hill and alongside Thirteenth Brook. At 3.3 miles you reach a junction with Beach Road, the gravel spur that leads in 0.6 miles to the large trailhead parking area at the end of the road, just a few hundred feet from Thirteenth Lake.

The Trail

Later in this book I will describe Thirteenth Lake as a canoe-camping option, and as you begin this trek to Hour Pond you will immediately understand why. The hiking trail begins as a recreational access path to a nearby beach on the northernmost tip of the lake, with several campsites clustered between the parking area and the water. This can be a busy place on summer weekends, and though Thirteenth Lake is not without leeches, the beach makes a great post-hike swimming spot.

The red-marked hiking trail, though, veers right and quickly leaves the graded access path behind. It narrows into a rugged foot trail and embarks on a 0.9-mile trek along the northwestern shoreline of the lake, with frequent views. All but a tiny corner of the lake is owned by the state, and you can see Garnet Hill Lodge up on one of the hills. The trail skirts around one designated campsite and cuts through another—options that are weighed a bit more closely in the canoe-camping section of this guidebook.

At 0.9 miles, the trail drops to a small canoe landing next to a large rock and a marker indicating campsite #9. At this point the foot trail veers inland and meets Peaked Mountain Brook at 1 mile, where the trails to Peaked Mountain and Hour Pond split company. The trail to Hour turns left to cross the brook, but this is a sizable stream that has resisted previous efforts to bridge it. Therefore hikers must step (or hop) from rock to rock—a feat best attempted in times of low water.

Across the stream, the trail resumes its prior course parallel to the shoreline, but now somewhat back from the water. The birches and aspens marking the extent of a past forest fire quickly transition to hemlocks and spruces—an unburned forest that will accompany you for the rest of the hike. This abrupt forest change suggests Peaked

Hour Pond. *Photo courtesy of the author*

Mountain Brook, devourer of footbridges, may have also served as a natural firebreak.

At 1.3 miles you reach a second junction, this one located within sight of the shoreline. The side trail to the left leads in about 130 feet to the shoreline trailhead where paddlers on Thirteenth Lake can access a designated campsite nearby, set back in the woods beside a small stream.

The trail to Hour Pond turns southwest and crosses the stream. This same stream becomes a trail companion as the footpath begins its climb away from the lake and into the nameless mountains. Soon it becomes engulfed by a rugged ravine, which the trail does its best to circumvent. For one brief moment, the trail traverses a narrow bench clinging to the side of the slope, with a sharp drop-off to your right—not a perilous spot, but one that enhances the sense of adventure.

An interesting interlude comes when the trail skirts a swampy basin hidden among the small summits. The final climb brings you to a height-of-land 470 feet above the lake, which is quickly followed by a descent to the southwest beside yet another small stream. It brings you to a third junction at 26 miles; the trail to the left is the original route from Old Farm Clearing.

Turn right, west. The trail leads to a pretty beaver pond at 2.7 miles where you will need to walk along the top of the long dam, which unlike many beaver dams seems purpose-built for the task; except in the wettest weather, it is a relatively easy traverse. The trail then traces a U-shaped course around the foot of one of the hills that provides Hour Pond its privacy, passing open wetlands and a dry streambed as it swings northwest toward your destination.

The trail does not lead directly to the water but, instead, continues to a former campsite about a third of the way up the shoreline, where it ends 3.5 miles from the Beach Road trailhead. This is an attractive spot with a good view across the pond to Bullhead Mountain, but the lean-to stands 500 feet to the north of this spot, at the end of a marked side trail. This shelter is located on high ground with a substantial setback from the water. A rock on the shoreline provides access to the pond.

Hour Pond appears relatively large, but it is remarkably shallow and therefore not very appealing for swimming, although it is a protected brook trout pond. In addition to the lean-to, there is also a well-used campsite to the south of the trail, not far from the pond's outlet.

7 Wilson Pond

Synopsis: A classic backpacking destination with challenging beaver meadows but a scenic payoff
Hiking Distance: 3 miles
Vertical Rise: 460 feet

Tiny Wilson Pond might not have ever become an obvious backpacking destination were it not for the lean-to on its north shore, which transformed this obscure trout pond into an attractive and popular hike. The lean-to exploits a rock ledge on the shoreline, revealing an enchanting view of remote Blue Ridge, an unimaginatively named mountain that forms the centerpiece of the namesake Blue Ridge Wilderness. It is a place to daydream—or to fish, if that is more your style. The visibility of the trailhead ensures this is a popular year-round hike.

A few caveats should be mentioned first. A few short sections of the trail can be hopelessly wet, and while these conditions have rarely turned people away, some of the obstacles are notable enough to recommend this as a dry-season hike—from late spring to early fall, say.

Second, the *only* camping option at Wilson Pond is the lean-to itself. Unlike many of the other lean-to sites described in this guide, there are no other legal campsites to serve as alternates should you arrive late only to find the shelter occupied. Many people visit Wilson just for the day, so a crowded parking area isn't necessarily an indicator the lean-to is full. Nevertheless, be sure to check the trailhead register to see how many people may be out ahead of you, and perhaps be prepared to select a different destination if you've arrived on a busy day.

Getting There

The trailhead is easily found on NY 28 by driving 2.7 miles west from the hamlet of Blue Mountain Lake. Prominent signs mark the turnout on the south side of the road, which provides ample parking.

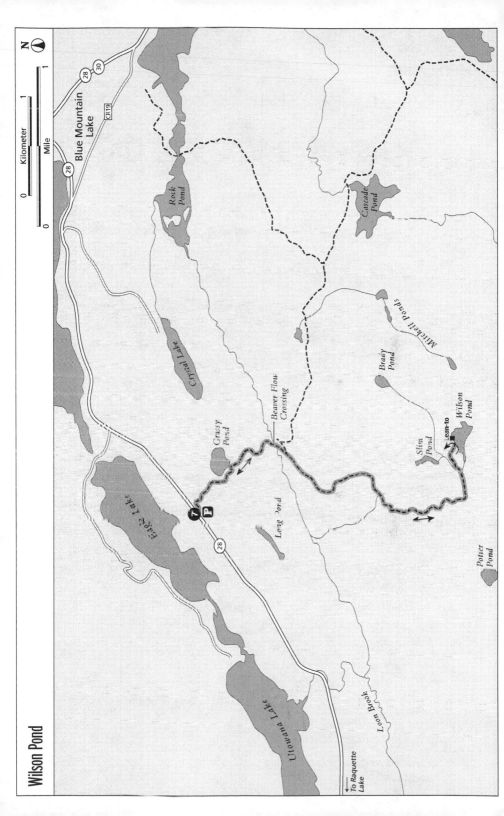

Wilson Pond

The Trail

One highlight of this hike is that nearly all of it passes through mature forests—few if any signs of past logging anywhere, even though much of the route follows the trace remains of an old wagon road.

From the parking area, the trail passes through a shady hemlock forest. Technically this first section is on private land, and the faint cross-trail encountered at 0.2 miles marks the state land boundary. If you miss these details, don't worry—there has traditionally been little signage to mark this event. Soon you will begin to spot Grassy Pond to the left, and at 0.5 miles you reach a bend in the trail where herd paths lead left into the bog to such scenic views as may be found here. Grassy Pond is round and lined with trees such as spruce, fir, and tamarack, but it is otherwise indifferent to the numerous hikers passing through trying to take pictures.

I mentioned the trail to Wilson Pond could be wet at times. The first encounter comes at the outlet of Grassy Pond, a tiny stream that resists containment; a haphazard array of logs and planks is humanity's best attempt at a bridge. A few minutes later the old roadbed (really a nice trail!) circles around to the foot of a beaver meadow that opens up to your right. For a brief time, the trail may be muddy or even partly submerged below the dam—problems in early spring perhaps, but less so in midsummer.

The most notorious obstacle, though, comes at 0.9 miles where a sprawling beaver flow fills the bottom of the next valley with no obvious way around. Fortunately for hikers there has always (somehow) been a feasible route directly through this wetland, although the exact location of that route has been slowly drifting downstream over the years as the beavers periodically reconfigure their dams. The current crossing is maybe 80 to 100 feet east of where it used to be when I first came this way, yet improbably it works. Thus my recommendation to come here in the summer, when this robust stream should be less of an issue.

Upon reaching the far shore, signs alert you to a little-used connector trail to Cascade Pond. The Wilson Pond trail bears right and hugs the edge of the wetland for about 200 feet, with fading signs marking

Beaver dam on the Wilson Pond Trail. *Photo courtesy of the author*

where past crossings used to terminate. Then it rejoins the old roadbed and begins the long climb up to the pond.

This next phase of the hike is characterized by a gentle but persistent ascent through tall hardwoods. Occasionally the tread is marred by mud or the erosion of a passing stream, but mostly the walking is easy. The roadbed eventually fades away, although it is difficult to pinpoint exactly where.

The final phase begins at 1.9 miles, where conifers crowd the trail and you are presented with your next stream crossing—a tributary of the beaver flow, but also the combined outlets of Slim, Brady, and Wilson Ponds. Again there is no bridge, only big rocks to serve as stepping stones. The trail then winds through the spruce-birch forest—a real delight. When the conifers again disperse to make way for the return of the hardwoods, the winding continues unabated. You may notice, though, that some of these bends are vertical, sharp ups and downs as the trail cuts against the topographical grain.

Somewhere off to your left is the wetland known as Slim Pond, although the glimpses of open space visible from the trail are the nameless wetlands located elsewhere on its outlet. After climbing up, over, and down five or so consecutive knolls, the trail finally bends east and descends to a stream crossing at 2.8 miles—a branch of the same stream you have already crossed twice before. This iteration is the outlet of Wilson Pond, and as before there is no bridge. If necessary there are stepping stones a short distance upstream.

The final push to the lean-to is a 0.2-mile jaunt through the cool shadows of a conifer forest. The shelter is approached from behind, standing roughly 50 feet back from the shoreline and turned at a ninety-degree angle from the water. An ovoid area around the lean-to roughly 200 feet long has been scavenged closely over the years for firewood, but beyond that signs of human passage fall off sharply. My favorite part of the shelter is the electrical outlet carved ironically into the wall.

Two paths lead out to the rock ledge, which offers the best water access. A tiny island partly obscures the view of Blue Ridge, but clearer views can be found from points east along the shore. Also, the pond's outlet trails off to the west into a rock-lined cove that is also worth seeing, for those people with an itch to explore once camp has been set up.

8 Cedar Lakes

Synopsis: Hike to a large lake with three remote lean-tos in a region teeming with history
Hiking Distance: 4.5 miles to northern lean-to; 5.2 miles to middle lean-to; and 7.6 miles to southern lean-to
Elevation Change: 600 feet in the first 2.2 miles but rolling terrain thereafter

The first question you may ask is this: Why does this singular lake have a plural name? It is a good question, but the lake will provide its own answer once you see the place.

Today the West Canada Lake Wilderness is the second-largest protected area in the northeastern United States, and like the High Peaks (the only wilderness that is larger) it shares a kinship of wetness. Although one region is mountainous and the other lake-studded, both rake substantial amounts of annual precipitation from the sky and therefore share comparable climates, soil structures, and forest cover. If the West Canadas were anywhere near as popular as the High Peaks, there would be many terabytes' worth of articles written about the hopelessness of trail erosion here as well, all for the same pedological reasons.

But for better or worse, this region does not receive the same scrutiny, even though enough history exists to fill an entire book dedicated to nothing but the region we now call the West Canada Lake Wilderness. This has been in many ways a contested terrain, perceived and used in different ways by different people at different times. The version enjoyed today, consisting of 172,000 motorless acres accessed almost exclusively by long gravel roads that are open for only half the year, did not fully come into being until the 1980s.

The hike to Cedar Lakes from the Pillsbury Mountain trailhead reveals aspects of this history to attentive hikers. The precise location of today's parking area was itself part of a public debate dating to 1983 and reflects a compromise struck between people who wanted no motorized access at all and others who understood the area to be a network of rugged logging roads and hidden hunting cabins. At that time, the days when floatplanes landed at will near the Cedar Lakes Ranger Station

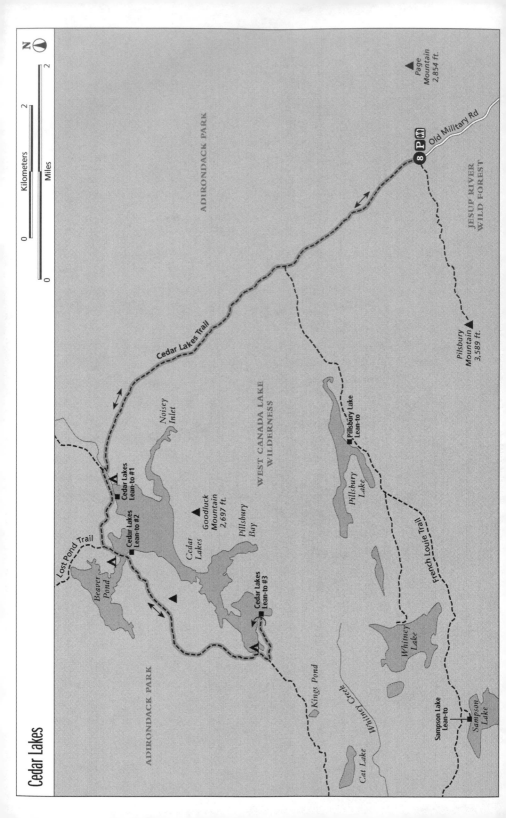

Cedar Lakes

N

Kilometers
0   2

Miles
0   2

ADIRONDACK PARK

Page Mountain 2,854 ft.

Old Military Rd

8 P A

JESUP RIVER WILD FOREST

Pilsbury Mountain 3,589 ft.

Cedar Lakes Trail

Noisey Inlet

WEST CANADA LAKE WILDERNESS

Pillsbury Lake Lean-to

Pillsbury Lake

Goodluck Mountain 2,697 ft.

Cedar Lakes Lean-to #1

Cedar Lakes Lean-to #2

Lost Pond Trail

Beaver Pond

Cedar Lakes

Pillsbury Bay

Cedar Lakes Lean-to #3

French Louie Trail

Whitney Lake

Kings Pond

ADIRONDACK PARK

Whitney Creek

Cat Lake

Sampson Lake Lean-to

Sampson Lake

were still a fresh memory, and to some people the area's conversion to wilderness status had not always been a foregone conclusion.

Historically, the Cedar Lakes were more or less as described: a chain of three distinct ponds plus neighboring Beaver Pond. They were forcibly united in the early twentieth century by a lumber dam, later replaced by a more permanent structure built by the state. And thus they remained until the early years of the current century, when natural erosion began to undercut the dam and allow water to slowly leak out every summer. Unlike Duck Hole, where the old dam suffered catastrophic failure in 2011, the Cedar Lakes are somewhat more like a leaky balloon: inflating every spring but deflated again by July. Meanwhile, the beavers over at Beaver Pond have formed their own breakaway republic, ensuring their arm remains fully flooded.

As a backpacking destination, Cedar Lakes is exceptional, although possessing a basic grasp of this human history will help you understand what you're seeing when you arrive. There are three lean-tos spaced out along its complicated shoreline, each providing its own distinct experience, plus a scattered collection of tent sites. The lake is moderately popular, and you will have human company through late summer and early fall, but the number of campsites does satisfy the current demand.

Getting There

The Pillsbury Mountain trailhead is also one of the most popular entry points for the wilderness interior, but it is located at the end of a rugged gravel road near Sled Harbor in the Perkins Clearing Tract. Follow NY 30 for 8.2 miles north of Speculator or 15.6 miles south of Indian Lake, where Perkins Clearing Road begins at an intersection near Mason Lake. Follow this road for 3.2 miles from NY 30, passing Mason Lake, and turn right onto Old Military Road, which crosses the Miami River 1.2 miles later and reaches a large clearing at 4.9 miles from NY 30. This is Sled Harbor, where low-clearance vehicles often park.

The road to the official trailhead, however, turns right at 5 miles. This is the continuation of Old Military Road. Not too long ago, it was barely passable to cars due to the rocks exposed on the slopes—especially one steep slope found near the beginning that was very eroded. The situation has improved somewhat, although having a high-clearance vehicle still helps, as the road is still prone to washouts after violent storms. Some people may elect to walk this first 1.2-mile section, which gently ascends 250 feet to the upper parking area. It takes no more than thirty minutes to walk to this point.

The Trail

The trail to Cedar Lakes is long, but the route is not complicated. From the Pillsbury Mountain trailhead at the end of Old Military Road, continue northwest along the barricaded extension of the road—now part of the wilderness and maintained as a foot trail. The width of the roadbed remains apparent even after decades of closure to motor vehicles, but hikers have worn only a narrow tread through the encroaching vegetation. The route is level at first but it soon begins to climb, aggressively so in one long, eroded section. This section tops out at 1.6 miles and 420 vertical feet at a gentle pass between Blue Ridge and Pillsbury Mountains. A trail to the left leads to Pillsbury Lake.

Continue straight for Cedar Lakes. In short order the trail (still an old road, much degraded by time) begins its northern descent from the pass. After the first and steepest slope you reach the site of a washed-out bridge over the aptly named Stony Brook, and at 2.2 miles you reach a reconstructed bridge over the equally aptly named Grassy Brook. (Stony and Grassy are the exact same stream, for some reason bestowed with separate names for its upland and lowland sections.)

The next 2 miles between Grassy Brook and the Cedar River is a long traverse along the foot of Noisey Ridge. The way is mostly level and sometimes wet, with sections of mossy conifers and gloomy hardwoods. At 4.2 miles you reach the south end of the Cedar Lakes Dam, such as it remains; the structure is mostly intact but is clearly old. Look for designated campsites in this area.

The trail makes a hairpin right turn at the dam and descends to a bridge over the Cedar River—a major tributary of the Hudson, although you would never guess from its small size here. Just beyond, at 4.3 miles, you reach an intersection with the Northville-Placid Trail (NPT).

Cedar Lakes shoreline. *Photo courtesy of the author*

Bear left to begin the enjoyable trek around the lakes. Your first glimpse of Cedar Lakes may be underwhelming, since the outlet end is a narrow channel that may reveal a lot of exposed ground in the summer. However, be faithful! The trail passes a choice campsite located on a small point, then passes a shoreline clearing with the ruins of an old root cellar—all that remains of the old ranger station, where a caretaker and his wife once spent their summers in pre-wilderness days.

The northernmost lean-to, Cedar Lakes No. 1, is just beyond, 4.5 miles from the trailhead. This site straddles the trail and is perhaps the most social of the three, a popular waypoint for NPT through-hikers. It stands in a small clearing of its own, with a path through the brush to the water. This is your first good look at the main lake, which even in low water is quite large.

Continuing west around the lake, turn left at a junction at 5 miles (where right goes to Lost Pond). A few minutes later, at 5.2 miles, you reach a particularly scenic area of some import. In addition to the views across the lake, where low water reveals a beach of sorts, there is a

Camping at Cedar Lakes No. 3 lean-to. *Photo courtesy of the author*

causeway and a bridge across the outlet of Beaver Pond. North of the bridge, look for a designated campsite to the right, tucked away in the woods. Across the bridge, an unmarked side trail leads right for 0.1 miles to a reliable spring. But more significantly is the side trail left, which leads 200 feet to the middle lean-to, Cedar Lakes No. 2. This one is perched well to take in the view across the lake, with Blue Ridge Mountain forming a prominent bulge on the horizon.

The next 1.8 miles are spent away from the shoreline and would otherwise be uneventful except for the traverse of Cobble Hill, with its tiring ascent and descent at each end. When next you see Cedar Lakes, you have arrived at a bay on the southernmost of the three lobes, a world apart from the north end. At 7 miles, look for herd paths leading left toward the water. The campsite here is distinguished by the metal rim of an old wagon wheel encircling the fireplace.

You reach a key junction at 7.2 miles—although I feel obligated to report that trail signs here have a history of disappearing. Whereas the NPT continues southwest toward the West Canada Lakes, the destination of this hike involves a left turn onto the side that may or may not be marked. Regardless, it is a well-worn trail that leads 0.4 miles east to the southernmost lean-to, Cedar Lakes No. 3.

This spot, 7.6 miles total from the trailhead, is the most solitary of the three shelters—that is, solitary in terms of distance from the main trail, not necessarily in usage. The lake is much smaller at this end; therefore, the views are more intimate than expansive. A crude dock on the shoreline marks the historic high-water mark when the dam was still fully functional.

9 West Stony Creek

Synopsis: Hike through the grand open woods of the southern Adirondacks to a streamside lean-to

Hiking Distance: 3.9 miles

Vertical Descent: Rolling terrain ending with a 540-foot descent

For many years, West Stony Creek was an unknown landmark. It flowed for several miles through a secluded valley near Benson, in the southernmost corner of Hamilton County, without drawing too much attention to itself. It was peaceful, unvisited, and perfectly wild.

In 2015, the Adirondack Mountain Club (ADK for short) realized its long-term goal of rerouting portions of the 130-mile-long Northville-Placid Trail (NPT). One priority was replacing an unpopular walk along Benson Road with a new trail to the south, in the Shaker Mountain Wild Forest. Inevitably, that trail led straight to West Stony, which has now become one of the through-trail's scenic highlights—and at some times of the year, one of its more notorious obstacles.

There is no bridge across West Stony. The creek is simply too wide, and its banks too low, for trail stewards to build anything but some mammoth suspension bridge. Currently, the only way to cross it is to take your boots off and ford—which at some times of the year is apt to be a cold and uncomfortable proposition.

But you don't need to ford West Stony to enjoy it as a hiking and camping destination. In 2018, the state built a lean-to on its north bank, making this an enticing destination for a weekend hike, and not just a route for through-hikers. Since it sits in the woods sheltered by hills on both sides of the creek, the lean-to seems even more remote than maps would suggest.

Fording the creek in high water can be tricky; therefore, I am recommending this out-and-back hike from the north, beginning at a popular trailhead on Benson Road. From here it is a 3.9-mile hike to the lean-to. There are hills in both directions, but the most notable is the 540-foot descent from the last height-of-land into the valley.

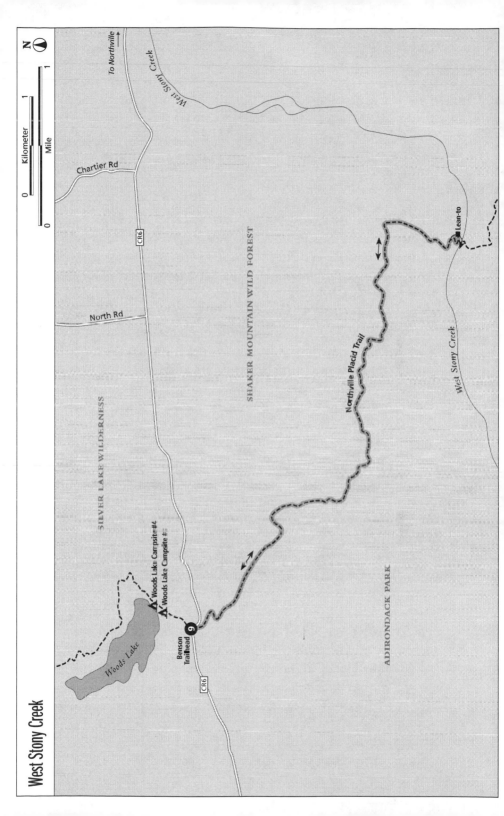

West Stony Creek

Getting There

To find Benson Road, follow NY 30 north from Northville for 3.3 miles. Benson Road, a county highway, leads west from this point through its namesake town. Follow it for 4.6 miles to the popular NPT parking area, located on the left side of the road.

The Trail

The trail to West Stony Creek begins at the east end of the parking area, dipping immediately through a hemlock-shaded glen. But then it climbs to the southeast, zigzagging about 200 vertical feet up the side of a hill and then contouring along it. There are hardwoods at first, and then glorious stands of hemlocks. In character, this area is essentially a southward extension of the Silver Lake Wilderness to the north, with forests just as grand and open. But if the forest pest known as the hemlock woolly adelgid ever finds its way to Benson, the effects on the area's iconic hemlock stands could be catastrophic.

There really are no landmarks to watch for along this hike; just enjoy the subtle changes in forest cover, the small hills, the tiny streams, and the rock outcrops. If you are following along on your map, you may notice that the trail is contouring along the first hill south of Benson Road, keeping to high ground until it descends and begins to traverse the broad plateau north of the creek. The forest is alternately shady hemlocks and open hardwoods. The latter sections feature some nice specimens of ash trees. These are currently healthy, but like the hemlocks they face the potential for extirpation as another invasive pest, the emerald ash borer, threatens the Adirondacks.

At 2.4 miles the NPT curves around a small swamp that is apt to be partially flooded this time of year. The trail keeps clear of the wetness, swinging right around the little woodland pond, then left, and then right to begin an ascent of another hill. Like the first ascent you encountered, the purpose of this one is to get you onto high ground, not to climb to the highest point.

There is a distinct forest change after passing the swamp. The soil seems shallower and rockier, and the hardwoods are less grand. Instead

West Stony Creek. *Photo courtesy of the author*

of northern hardwoods like maple and yellow birch, there are now more poplars and red oaks. These will accompany you all the way to West Stony. The combination of the rocks and the forest cover change suggest that a long-ago wildfire swept through this area, perhaps originating at one of Benson's old farms and extending southward until encountering the creek, a natural firebreak.

At 2.9 miles the trail passes a rocky knoll that *almost* offers a view of the valley toward which you are walking. I say "almost" because the knoll is not bare, although when the leaves are gone in the fall you can sense the distant hills.

The final descent begins slowly at first, almost imperceptibly. The trail heads east, but then at 3.3 miles it makes a sharp turn to the right, south. Now you are like a plane coming in for a landing, making a long approach into the valley. The way is never steep, but the trail is rockier here than at any other point since leaving Benson. It drops more than 300 feet in the final 0.6 miles, reaching the creek at 3.9 miles.

West Stony Creek is not very deep—in summer you can step across the exposed cobbles without ever getting your feet wet—but it is remarkably wide; the continuing trail on the south bank is about 150 feet away. The north bank is almost entirely forested with hardwoods, particularly beech, oak, and poplar. The south bank is a wall of evergreens, mostly hemlocks. Long, narrow meadows grace each bank, kept clear of tree saplings by the buildup of ice every winter. The best time to view these meadows is late summer, when they are ablaze with wildflowers.

A sign points left, east, to the lean-to. The lean-to stands about 300 feet off the main trail and 200 feet back from the water. There is no view, but it is a fine place to take shelter from the cold weather. The devastated patch of forest a short distance away was not the result of a site-specific tornado, but an artificial clearing created by the Department of Environmental Conservation to drop in the lean-to materials by air.

PART II
PRIMITIVE TENT SITES

As numerous as the lean-tos are, they are easily outnumbered by the vast array of primitive tent sites available throughout Adirondack Park. These are simple camping areas with few amenities, but they come in so many varieties that no two are exactly alike.

To enjoy these sites, one must be willing to forgo more than a few comforts of daily living. Yet it would be incorrect to call this "roughing it," as many people do. For people who enjoy the outdoors, the experience of camping out in the backcountry feels more like "cutting back to the essentials." At least for a time; alas, the sun rises and a new day arrives, and before long you are breaking camp and heading back to civilization.

Attempting to write a guide to every possible campsite one might want to visit would be a futile project, and the result would be a book as unwieldly as an old-fashioned telephone directory. (Remember those?) Instead, I faced another challenge when preparing for this book: selecting eight separate destinations that represent various aspects of Adirondack Park, but which provide distinct adventures from the nine previously described in the lean-to section.

The truth is, there are campsites in every part of the park, but many exist on trail systems that also lead to lean-tos. I could write about a wilderness lake that boasts both a pleasant campsite *and* a lean-to, and then try to fulfill my obligation by hyping up the campsite, but that is not what I am trying to accomplish.

Camping at East Pond. *Photo courtesy of the author*

Instead, this section is a listing of eight destinations with good camp-sites, where lean-tos are not even an option. Rather than being used out of obstinacy, the campsite is itself the anticipated destination—a place that is sought out for its own merits, and not just as the booby prize for people who arrived too late to snag the shelter.

Also, these are campsites that are easy to find. Like the lean-tos, these tent sites are well used and directly accessible from the trails that lead to them. No searching about should be required, which is a common trait among many of the more "secretive" sites in the Adirondacks.

Any good campsite will have plenty of level ground for at least one tent, access to water, something compelling to look at (if not directly from the campsite, then from a spot very close by), and a source of good firewood. With all of these criteria in mind, here is the list of outings I selected. I hope you enjoy.

10 Chub Lake

Synopsis: An exceptional campsite in an area that gets overlooked
Hiking Distance: 3 miles
Elevation Change: Rolling terrain

I blame the parking—or, rather, the lack thereof. This is the main reason why I think Chub Lake in the Pigeon Lake Wilderness doesn't get the love one might expect.

The hike that I am about to describe has its flaws, but all of these are worth overcoming. The trailhead may be a private driveway without a designated parking area for the public, and the trail may be obnoxiously wet in places, but the trade-off is a chance to hike through old-growth forests past one charming pond on your way to another. And the campsite at the destination is a classic, perched atop a rock ledge with an unimpeded view of the pond.

But yes, traffic is moderate to light on much of this trail, perhaps because the start is not obviously marked as an entrance to state land. Be aware that this trail begins on private land, and the right-of-way to access the wilderness does not include the right to leave the designated corridor or to drive the private road.

Getting There

From NY 28 in Eagle Bay, turn northwest onto Big Moose Road and follow it for 3.8 miles. Here, bear right onto Higby Road and continue for another 1.3 miles to the start of Judson Road, a gated private road on your right. Although there are few signs, this is an authorized access point for state land. Leave your car parked on the shoulder, being careful not to block the driveway.

The Trail

Beginning at the Judson Road gate, follow the private lane for 0.2 miles, watching for the well-marked fork where the public hiking trail veers right into the woods. It begins by following a section of Constable

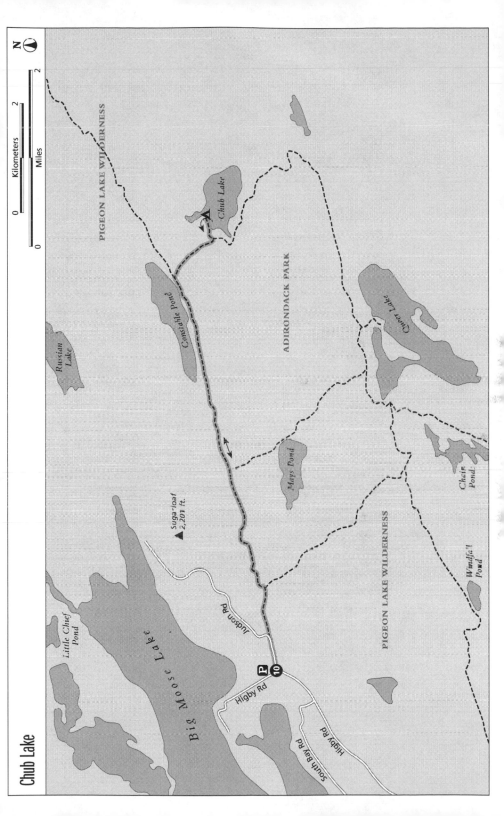

Chub Lake

Creek (a feature you will encounter more than once), reaching the state land boundary moments later. Even on good days the trail may be muddy, but at 0.5 miles you reach a junction with a trail to the right that cuts over to Queer Lake. For Chub, bear left across the bridge over the creek.

This interlude on state land is brief, and soon you reenter private land—with ample signage to inform you precisely when. At 0.9 miles the hiking trail intersects another gravel road and turns right to follow it across a second bridge over Constable Creek. As soon as you reach the far side, look for the trail signs pointing left back into the woods.

Although you are done with the roads, the muddiest sections are encountered in the next half mile. This is not a new development; the trail has been this way as long as I've known it. This is an unfortunate distraction, and a defect that could be easily remedied, if someone were to ever invest the time and resources. Nevertheless, it isn't all bad, and remember there are better times ahead.

At 1.3 miles you cross back into state land—this time for good—just before reaching a second trail junction. The route to the right leads to Mays Pond, but you want the trail that continues straight ahead. This is a narrow path through a rich forest, never known to be logged. The state acquired this land in 1897 as part of the settlement for a lawsuit with a private landowner and would-be lumber baron, who was frustrated in his ambitions by the creation of Stillwater Reservoir several miles to the northwest. His loss was the public's gain, and the trees still grow as big as they did before the invention of the automobile.

Eventually Constable Creek widens into Constable Pond, which you can glimpse at several points along the trail—although the path never quite approaches the shoreline. What side paths you do see leading down to the water were probably worn by hungry beavers venturing inland in search of fresh wood. The one exception comes at 2.5 miles, when you finally reach the junction with the side trail to Chub Lake. Before you make that turn, set down your backpack for a moment and venture in the opposite direction, toward Constable. The crudest of herd paths leads down to a spot on the shore where a rock tucked away in the grasses and shrubs provides the best view I've ever found

Chub Lake campsite. *Photo courtesy of the author*

of this pond. Graceful pines sprout up from random points all along Constable's long shorelines.

Turning southeast on the Chub Lake trail, you climb gently past a wetland for 0.4 miles and arrive at another T-intersection. This time turn left onto the deadend side trail to Chub Lake's highly attractive campsite, located 3 miles from Higby Road.

There are several reasons to recommend this site: there is space for several tents, a well-sited fireplace, and a ledge with a view that is hard to argue with. Chub Lake is a circular pond with a protected brook trout fishery. Once you reach this spot you may find it hard to leave.

11 Big Pond

Synopsis: An easy hike with an optional side trip to big mountain views
Hiking Distance: 1.7 miles
Elevation Change: Rolling terrain

The Hoffman Notch Wilderness often tends to be an afterthought in discussions of the Adirondacks. At 38,000 acres it is actually fairly significant in size, and it is further distinguished by a range of large mountains. The interior is well forested, and no one doubts the wildness of those hidden valleys and tremendous slopes.

However, in strictly anthropocentric terms, it pales as a recreational asset when compared to such nearby gems as the Pharaoh Lake Wilderness to the east and the High Peaks to the north—places that are so jam-packed full of trails and campsites and lean-tos that no introduction in this guidebook seems warranted. Rather, Hoffman Notch is the middle child in this family arrangement: perfectly upstanding in every meaningful way, but constantly overlooked.

This history of oversight is as old as Adirondack Park itself. When the original Blue Line was established in 1892, it excluded parts of what is now the eastern boundary of the wilderness, probably signifying that at the time these were still inhabited areas. Eighty years later, state land planners were on the fence as to whether Hoffman Notch should be wilderness; there were snowmobile trails here at the time, and it was not until 1972 that the decision was made to remove the motors and protect the landscape.

In more recent times backpackers have neglected the place, due largely to a dearth of campsites. One of Hoffman Notch's quirks is that its most attractive destinations (other than the notch itself) lie in peripheral parts of the wilderness, so close to the entry points that they hardly seem "backcountry." However, this perception may change in the near future as the North Country National Scenic Trail (NCNST) is strung through the southern portion of the area, creating an east-west hiking corridor through the park (and beyond).

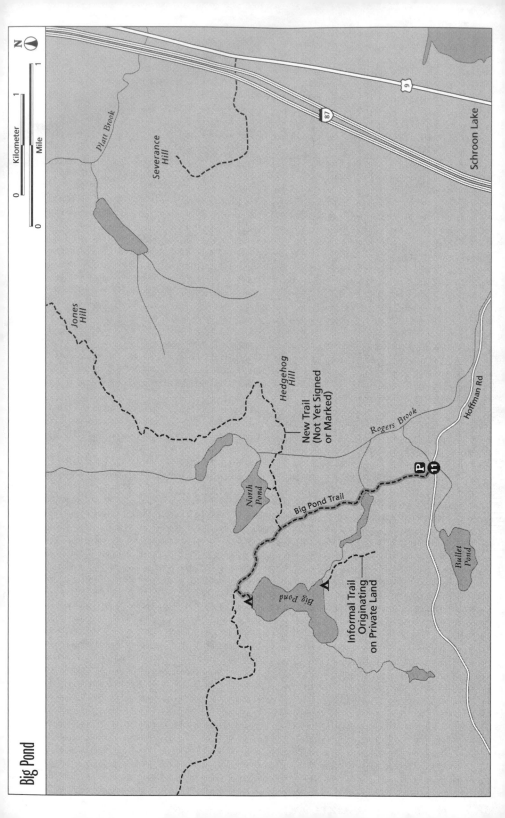

Big Pond

Big Pond, located in the southeastern corner of the wilderness, will be a prominent waypoint on that trail. It is also a popular day-hiking destination, and although there is a prime campsite on the pond's north end, most visitors probably only stay long enough to soak in the view. It remains to be seen whether the new through-trail (not yet complete as of this writing) will significantly change these usage patterns, but in the meantime if you are searching for a short overnight getaway not far from a town with services, Big Pond is hard to beat.

Getting There

This entrance to the Hoffman Notch Wilderness is located just a few miles west of Schroon Lake, a lively town with many services and good restaurants, all of it easily accessible from Interstate 87 (also known as the Adirondack Northway).

From Exit 28, drive south on US 9 through the village to Hoffman Road, a right turn. Hoffman Road crosses the Northway and climbs into the foothills, eventually reaching the trailhead 2.1 miles from town. It is located on the right, with room for about two or three cars to park.

The Trail

This trail follows an old woods road and provides an easy walk, as wilderness hikes go, beginning in a plantation of pine and ending in a native stand of hemlock. What hills do exist are almost imperceptible until the very end.

The hike begins beside an old cellar hole hidden next to the parking area. If this weren't a big enough clue, the even-aged pine forest surrounding the start of the trail should further suggest that much of this area was once a cleared farm, many years ago. The trail leads to a wide bridge across a rather boisterous branch of Rogers Brook at 0.5 miles, your first landmark of the day. The bridge is located at the foot of a long beaver flow that is not without scenic interest of its own, and if you investigate a short distance downstream you will find some interesting cascades. (If your itinerary leaves room for side explorations on this otherwise brief adventure, stick a pin in this location and read the section that follows.)

Big Pond. *Photo courtesy of the author*

After the bridge, the trail angles northwest through the rolling terrain, still clearly following an ancient roadbed. Curiously, whoever picked this route in a prior century managed to thread the needle well between two of the area's most scenic assets: Big Pond and North Pond, heading directly between both without a glimpse of either. The new North Country Trail segment will resolve that problem, but it is still curious how the original trail seems intent to keep these "secrets" safe.

After less than an hour of hiking, there is a swift but subtle change in both the trail and its surrounding environment. The old road comes to an end, and the trail continues as a narrower footpath. At around the same time, the second-growth forest transitions to something more stately, with impressive hemlocks crowning a complicated network of knolls (probably of glacial origin). All of this amounts to something like a drastic mood change, cheered by the timely arrival of a stately forest more befitting a wilderness setting.

The most noteworthy hills also appear in this late section. After climbing one hemlock knoll and descending the other side, be on the alert for a trail junction. At a point 1.6 miles from Hoffman Road a side trail veers left—an obvious turn even if the signage is minimal. The main trail continues straight ahead into the headwater region of Trout Brook, but the left trail leads in just 0.1 miles to the well-situated campsite perched above a pebbly beach. It is an ideal location, especially since it faces into the sun and overlooks most of this wild pond.

Side Trips

The hike to Big Pond is fine for people who enjoy easy hikes or are short on time, but a quick glance at a map shows other options exist nearby as well.

A new section of the NCNST leading over Jones Hill is mostly cut and ready to explore, though as of this writing (2023) it is not yet officially opened. Presumably the addition of signs and markers in the near future will make the junction with the existing trail described earlier abundantly obvious, and backpackers with a yen to go climb something will definitely want to check this out. The new trail passes south of North Pond—with its fine views of Hoffman Mountain—and then circles through the foothills to flank Jones Hill from the southwest. After a quick climb, the trail-to-be follows the ridgeline to what has already become a favorite summit view for local hikers already in the know.

Backing up to the beaver flow on the unnamed Rogers Brook tributary mentioned earlier, interesting off-trail adventures are possible here as well. For instance, you can bushwhack along the north bank of the beaver pond a short distance west to glimpse one of the most active heron rookeries in the area. The flow is larger than it appears on maps, and the rookery is located on a collection of snags rising from the water. Without a canoe there is little danger you will get too close to the nests and become a nuisance to the local residents.

And if you are persistent enough to find someplace truly off the beaten path, the south shore of Big Pond features a second campsite, this one much more hidden than the first but featuring views that are far more photogenic, including Hoffman and its range of fellow mountains. This site is on state land but is not connected to the main trail network; therefore, it can only be reached legally by skirting off-trail around the north side of the sprawling beaver flow. Just be aware that ticks are lurking in the leaf litter.

12 Indian Lake and the Indian River

Synopsis: Scout a future section of a long-distance hiking trail while use still remains low

Hiking Distance: 2.4 miles to Indian Lake; 4.4 miles to the Indian River

Elevation Change: Rolling terrain

Nature is not static, and neither are the schemes designed by humans to manage it. This adventure is an illustration of the ability of the wilderness to reclaim such pesky intrusions as roads and rustic campsites, for reasons I will point out in a moment. But not only that, this is a damn good backpacking trip in a region that for most people has fallen off the map.

A national economic crisis that began in 2008 hit New York's state government especially hard due to its reliance on corporate tax income from Manhattan-based firms, forcing it to cut budgets for several years to come. Agencies across the board were expected to drop costly programs, and some of the results were expected (such as state parks temporarily closing due to staffing shortages) while others seemed somewhat random (such as the Department of Transportation shuttering highway rest stops).

Here in the Adirondacks, one of the practical effects of that recession was the ultimate closure of a remote road deep within the Moose River Plains. But not right away, though. This route was located in an area that in the 1960s had been the subject of a series of spectacular land acquisitions, resulting in the addition of what is now the Moose River Plains Wild Forest to the roster of Forest Preserve lands, as well as the creation of a "recreation area" strung out along an extensive network of former logging roads throughout those tracts.

As part of its belt-tightening measures, the Department of Environmental Conservation (DEC) temporarily ceased the costly maintenance of certain Forest Preserve roads, including all of those within the Moose River Plains. However, local county road crews quickly stepped up to keep the recreation area open, as best they could. Nevertheless the remotest road in the area, Indian Lake Road, was eventually deemed not worth the financial cost for continued maintenance, and in a management-planning decision made a few years later, the DEC decided to close a portion of it permanently.

I last drove to Indian Lake late in 2010; the road was barricaded after the following season and has remained that way ever since. But when I returned on foot, the results were gratifying: within a remarkably short amount of time, the gravel surface had started to turn green with new vegetation and was reverting to the appearance of a trail, all on its own.

This may sound like a gimmick of a hike, but backpacking to Indian Lake is a better experience than you might expect. In fact, this closed road is slated to become part of the North Country National Scenic Trail (NCNST), making it a distant cousin to the Appalachian Trail. As a result, this may someday become a more highly trafficked route, and indeed a few NCNST markers are already in place—although the DEC has never completed a management plan for the adjacent West Canada Lake Wilderness, a prerequisite to building any new trail links; therefore, there is still time to savor the solitude of this area while it remains disconnected from other trail segments.

There is one other thing I ought to mention: Natural features with pejorative toponyms have been renamed—especially and including places named "Squaw." While the federal government replaced all such place names throughout the country in 2022, that specific effort has not yet reached the Adirondacks in terms of maps, signage, and so forth. Here I use both the new name and the old name simultaneously, for example, Muskrat (Squaw) Lake, with the former name in parentheses.

Getting There

The Moose River Plains is a popular recreation area with long gravel roads and numerous roadside campsites. If you have never visited this area before, be sure to check out the map of the road network posted at the entrance gate; likely you will be intrigued by all the campsites and trailheads you will be passing as you venture into one of the remotest parts of the area.

Note that these roads are notoriously bumpy, and the speed limit is a low 15 miles per hour. However, during the summer four-wheel-drive

Indian Lake and the Indian River

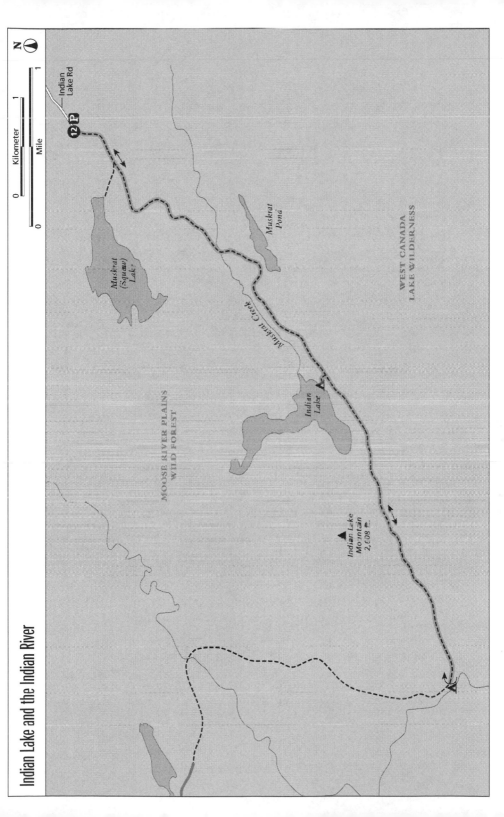

is not a requirement. The gates are open in time for Memorial Day and are closed at the end of hunting season, although no plowing occurs in the fall, and after Columbus Day four-wheel-drive *is* a requirement.

Beginning at NY 28 near the hamlet of Inlet, follow Limekiln Road south for 1.9 miles to the Moose River Plains entrance on the left (mile 0.0). At the first intersection 4.7 miles from the gate, turn left over the Red River. You reach the Plains proper—characterized by an expanse of brush with few trees—at 8.5 miles; here you should continue straight at a prominent intersection. You cross the South Branch Moose River at 9.7 miles and Otter Brook at 11.8 miles. The final barricade is at 14.7 miles, where there is room for several cars to park.

The Trail

The first 0.3 miles of this former road/new trail are quite well used, and the tread remains wide. However, once you reach the side trail to Muskrat (Squaw) Lake, located 0.2 miles downhill to the right, the worn treadway veers in that same direction. This is the best indication that the continuing roadway sees much less foot traffic.

A moment after Muskrat (Squaw) Lake you begin to encounter the first of the former roadside campsites, several of which were abandoned along with the road. The road makes a good walking surface, and the miles melt away swiftly. At 1.6 miles an old side trail (now barely discernible) leads left to a view of Muskrat Pond, about 160 feet away, and at 2 miles the old road dips through a low area that has long been prone to flooding.

At 2.4 miles you reach the former parking area near Indian Lake, where a side trail leads right for about 365 feet to the south shore. The lake's best campsite, once a walk-in site but now still perfectly valid for backpacking, is off to the right. Indian Lake is shaped somewhat like a boot, placing the campsite underneath its heel. Like many lakes in this region Indian was acidified and fishless for many years, although loons returned long ago and the place is no longer as "dead" as it once was.

Just beyond the old parking area is a second barricade, marking the site of an even older road closure. As recently as the 1970s, the public could continue driving the former logging road as far as the Indian

Indian Lake. *Photo courtesy of the author*

River, but when the river was added to the West Canada Lake Wilderness in 1979, the new boundary was drawn at this point.

As a result, the next 2 miles of roadway are even more trail-like. It remains a gentle route, troubled at times by encroaching beaver ponds and the neglect of fallen logs, but otherwise it remains a satisfying hiking route. It begins a long descent toward the river, and at 4.3 miles you have your first glimpse of the seldom-seen Indian.

A side path leads left off the road at 4.4 miles to the site of one of the old drive-in campsites from the 1970s, still lovingly (but lightly) used as a backpacking campsite. Is this the most exquisite campsite in the Adirondacks? No, but it practically oozes solitude, and the river access it provides is good.

This particular Indian River is 15.1 miles long, beginning as the outlet of Brooktrout Lake and ending as a tributary to the South Branch Moose River. For that entire distance, it exists as a free-flowing river without even so much as a bridge to spoil the scenery. If a place as wild and free as *this* isn't worth seeing, I don't know what is.

The trail does not end here and, in fact, continues even deeper into the wilderness as far as Horn Lake—a bit more of a hike than should be accommodated in a single overnight.

13 Upper Sargent Pond

Synopsis: Family-friendly outing to a scenic campsite
Hiking Distance: 1.2 miles
Elevation Change: Relatively level

Sometimes the best getaways are the easiest ones, and the outing to Upper Sargent Pond from North Point Road is so easy it is almost unbelievable such places exist. This is a straightforward hike to a beautiful campsite, about which not much more need be said.

Getting There

From NY 30 south of Long Lake, turn southwest onto North Point Road, following the signs for Buttermilk Falls and the Forked Lake Campground. Drive past both those landmarks (stopping for the quick walk to Buttermilk Falls on the Raquette River if time and inclination allow) to the Upper Sargent Pond trailhead at 6.2 miles, located on the left.

The Trail

I selected this outing because it provides balance to some of the meatier hikes I have been writing about elsewhere in these pages. There is really little to say about this trail; it leads south from the road and passes through a mature forest with more than a few noteworthy yellow birch trees; what climbing and descending does occur is so minimal it's not worth mentioning. In roughly 30 minutes you reach a junction with a side trail leading right toward Lower Sargent Pond, the largest and most popular in the three-pond chain. But for now you want to keep left, proceeding all the way to the end of the trail and the prominent campsite on Upper Sargent's north shore.

Scenery-wise, it would be difficult to expect more from a backcountry campsite. This spot is characterized by an open grassy patch with rocks along the shore and plenty of sun exposure—especially in the morning. (Hint: don't let yourself sleep in and miss the sunrise!) The

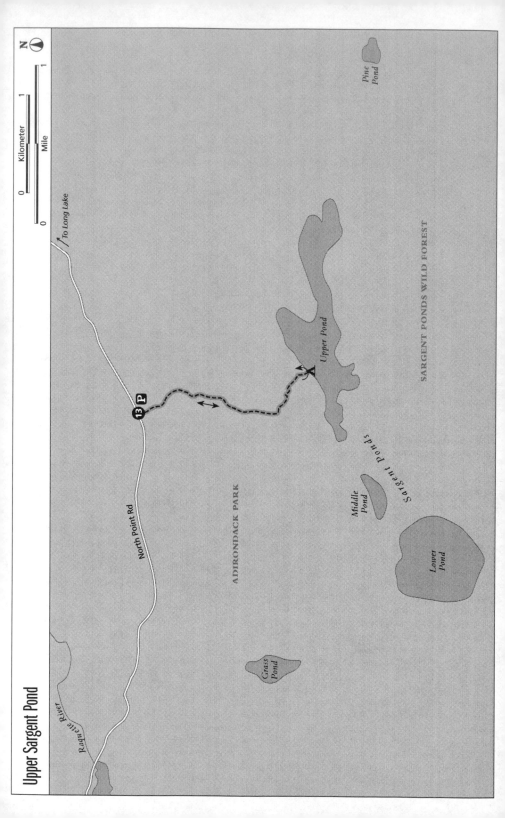

Upper Sargent Pond

N

Kilometer
0   1

Mile
0   1

To Long Lake

Raquette River

North Point Rd

13 **P**

ADIRONDACK PARK

Grass Pond

Middle Pond

Sargent Ponds

Lower Pond

Upper Pond

SARGENT PONDS WILD FOREST

Pine Pond

Morning at Upper Sargent Pond. *Photo courtesy of the author*

fireplace is backed up against one of the rocks, providing a much better venue for evening entertainment than any TV ever could.

In short: If you pick your evening well, this short trip could someday form the basis of some of your biggest memories.

14 Ross and Whortleberry Ponds

Synopsis: Hike a branching trail network to three ponds with excellent campsites at two

Hiking Distance: 2.7 miles to Ross Pond; 3.3 miles to Whortleberry Pond

Elevation Change: Rolling terrain

Years ago, the branching trail network to Ross, Whortleberry, and Big Bad Luck Ponds near Indian Lake was one of my first hiking and writing assignments for Barbara McMartin, the long-time Adirondack guidebook author who got me started in this field. At that time, 2001, this was a newly designated trail, as yet unknown to most people. The camping and fishing possibilities at each of the ponds made this an attractive place to visit, in addition to the scenic qualities of the area. Judging by the traffic at the trailhead parking area over the subsequent years, the trio of backcountry ponds enjoyed a modest following.

Then, in 2014, the state cut a new trail to OK Slip Falls, connecting this same trailhead to a recently acquired parcel in the Hudson River Gorge. The waterfall (a terrific day-hiking destination!) has proven to be so popular that the trailhead itself was rebranded as the OK Slip Falls Trailhead. The ponds, it seems, have been forgotten.

Still, I have a lingering fondness for the three ponds and have paid them several visits. Ross and Whortleberry have the best backpacking campsites, although neither is very big and the surrounding topography does little to block traffic sounds from NY 28, despite the distance. Both are great destinations, although the little campsite perched on the rock ledge at the east end of Whortleberry Pond has to be one of the prettiest I have seen.

Getting There

The trailhead parking area can be found on NY Route 28, 7.8 miles east of the intersection with NY Route 30 in Indian Lake, at a fork with an unnamed side road. You will need to walk westward along the shoulder of the highway for 0.2 miles to find the sign for the start of the trail.

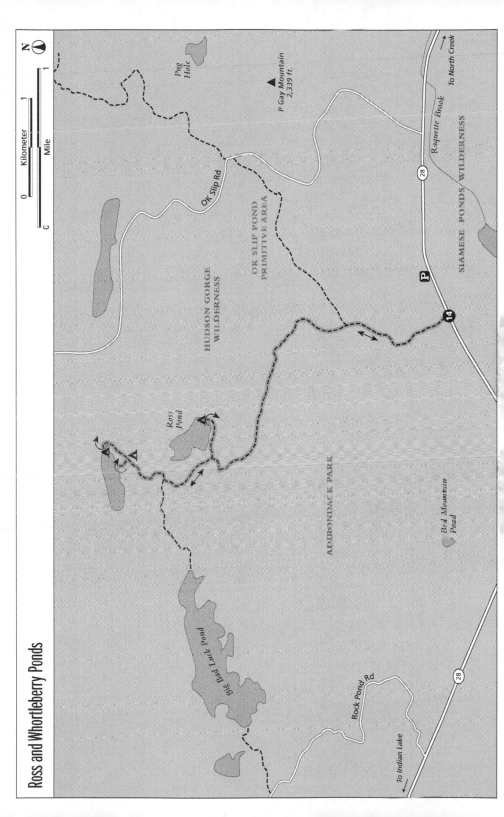

Ross and Whortleberry Ponds

The Trail

The trail to Ross, Whortleberry, and Big Bad Luck Ponds shares a common trailhead with the route to OK Slip Falls, which may be the most prominent listing on the trailhead guideboards. After walking down the highway shoulder to the trailhead at 0.2 miles, begin by following the trail down the berm and through a short muddy area, intercepting an old road within minutes. Bear right and follow the marked foot trail for 0.9 miles, over a small hill to a junction where the new blue-marked trail to OK Slip bears right.

The trail up to this point has become a well-worn route ever since the OK Slip purchase. The old trail to the left seems like a faint wilderness track by comparison, although it is marked and relatively easy to follow. It follows the trace of an old roadbed north and downhill into the valley of Bell Mountain Brook. This stream, which you reach at 1.3 miles, does not have a legitimate bridge but is easy enough to cross; on a spring visit once, I kept my boots dry by stepping on an assortment of small logs placed somewhat tenuously in a bridge-like position. It wasn't pretty, but it worked.

The trail then embarks on its longest climb, rising 220 feet in 0.4 miles to a rugged little notch with rock outcrops. A prolonged descent follows, with the trail passing close to beaver meadows that appear forlorn and muddy with their dams in disrepair. The trail circles through a muddy area with a few stepping stones erratically placed, and at 2.4 miles you reach the junction with the side trail to Ross Pond.

Here you have a choice to make: which campsite do you want? In terms of finding and accessing a site with the least amount of hassle, the one at Ross is by far the best option. The side trail is 0.3 miles long and loops around the south end of the pond to a campsite perched near rock ledges at the southeast corner. It is spacious and scenic, and comes with the added benefit of being located directly on the trail.

To continue to Whortleberry, follow the trunk trail northwest, dipping through a glen and reaching the side trail to Big Bad Luck Pond at 2.8 miles.

This side trail is 0.7 miles long and is definitely worth a look if you have time, although it does not lead to any campsites. Big Bad Luck is

Whortleberry Pond. *Photo courtesy of the author*

the largest of the three ponds, and its shores are rich with pine. However, trails stop short of reaching the main body of the lake, and the only way to reach its two excellent campsites is by boat.

Still following the main trail to Whortleberry, watch for a right turn 0.1 miles later; the trail is arcing northeast through a coniferous forest, but an unmarked trail continues straight, enticing you to stray in the wrong direction. Trail markers are notably scarce.

The rest of the hike passes through a thick forest of spruce, balsam, and pine, with the marked trail ending at 3.1 miles at a campsite in a rocky clearing—a legitimate place to pitch your tent, though not the one I'm recommending. You are very close to Whortleberry Pond at this point, although you can barely see it from here.

There are two ways to proceed. The shortest route to the shoreline is an unmarked path that leads northwest and downhill for about 250 feet to the pond's southern shore. This area is wooded and boggy, and the view of the pond will entice you to seek out something better.

The better option used to be to follow another unmarked trail leading northeast from the campsite for 0.2 miles. I speak in the past tense because beaver flooding has the potential to cut off easy foot access to the scenic campsite sitting atop a hemlock-covered ledge at the east end of the pond, 3.3 miles from the parking area. The well-used path led toward the outlet of the pond, crossed it, and then hooked west to reach the campsite. Northern Frontier, the nearby youth camp on OK Slip Pond, keeps a small fleet of boats stashed on the south bank of the outlet, presumably to make this crossing easier. Otherwise, the traditional way of dealing with beaver flooding is to seek out the dam and see if that can serve as a bridge.

The site features two scenic ledges. One is located high off the water, and the other dips down to its edge. Whortleberry is not a large pond, and you can see just about all of it from the campsite. Nor is it quite as remote as it might seem; loud trucks on the highway, and occasional activity at Northern Frontier, can all be heard.

This region also boasts several additional ponds to explore, well beyond the end of the marked trail, including a few that were opened to the public as part of the OK Slip Falls acquisition. The promise of additional explorations is enough to entice anybody back multiple times.

15 Blue Ledge on the Hudson River

Synopsis: Camp on one of the wildest parts of the Hudson River
Hiking Distance: 2.3 miles
Vertical Descent: 275 feet

During the height of the Adirondack fall foliage season, the intuitive notion for most hikers is to climb up—as in to the summit of a mountain, from which to survey a colorful landscape. There is nothing wrong with that way of thinking, but sometimes it's important to remember that wildness is something you can also descend into.

I've been reminded of this the last few years while I've indulged an infatuation with the Hudson Gorge Wilderness, the 22,906-acre bulge of state land along the Hudson River's wildest section. While there are peaks that one could climb in this region, one inevitably hikes down to reach the star feature, the Hudson Gorge itself. And when you visit in the fall, it's like being immersed in color; towering hardwoods fill the gorge, and when you are down by the river you feel awash in yellows and reds.

Of course, you can hike here in any season you please. People typically penetrate this rugged stretch of river by foot at only a few places, one of them being the 2.3-mile-long trail to Blue Ledge accessed via Northwoods Club Road near Minerva, New York. Blue Ledge is a towering cliff of steel-colored rock that hovers over a bend in the river, where artist Winslow Homer once painted watercolor scenes of lumbermen floating spruce logs through the gorge in the nineteenth century. The sandy banks are a natural gathering place, and on summer weekends they fill up with hikers and whitewater rafting parties.

This trail is available for most of the year despite its remote location, although expect seasonal road closures in early spring—Northwoods Club Road is graded annually but can be a little hairy after the snows melt. Although most people are day hikers—few seem inclined to bring an overnight backpack—there is an exceptional campsite about 100 feet downstream of the trail, spacious enough for several tents but offering a modicum of privacy.

Blue Ledge on the Hudson River

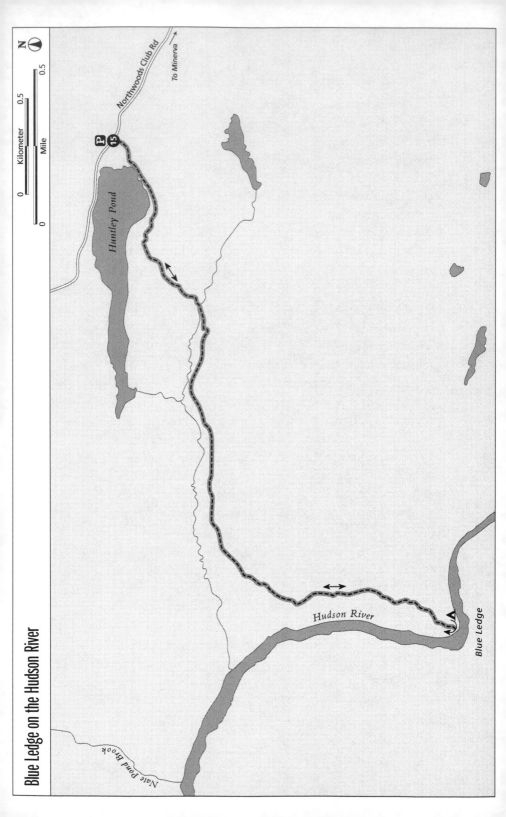

There are quirks about the river that anyone visiting in the peak summer tourist seasons should know, however. Because the river is a prize of the local whitewater industry, the Town of Indian Lake releases water from the dam at Lake Abanakee during the middle of the day. This creates a "bubble" of water to enhance the rafting experience, which would otherwise be slow and tedious to navigate in midsummer.

Thus, there are two implications for visitors in July and August: expect the water to rise quickly in the middle of the day, and a few minutes later expect to have dozens of visitors when the rafting parties arrive. The sand beaches at Blue Ledge are a favorite lunch stop for the outfitters, and for a brief while the gorge may seem either jovial or crowded, depending on your disposition.

Getting There

Finding the trailhead requires patience with long, winding roads, but the results are worth the effort. Follow NY 28N for 2.5 miles north of Minerva and turn left (west) onto Northwoods Club Road. This begins as an ordinary residential road, but soon the pavement ends and you enter state land. A narrow descent leads to the Boreas River at 3.8 miles, and after a long climb you descend again toward Huntley Pond. The trailhead for Blue Ledge is found just before the pond, 6.8 miles from the highway. Parking is on the right and the trail is on the left.

The Trail

The trail to Blue Ledge goes through several phases, but it begins as a pondside path plagued with fits of wetness, beginning with a long muddy section with unsatisfactory (and ineffective) attempts at bog bridging.

But don't stop reading just yet. After a few enchanting views of Huntley Pond, the trail pulls away from the shore and climbs briefly to a height-of-land at about 1,625 feet—the summit of this trail, already encountered just a few minutes into the trip. Then it cuts between a pair of boulders and descends to a small stream. Depending on water levels you can step across on stones or take advantage of the log bridge.

Blue Ledge campsite. *Photo courtesy of the author*

Next comes a long, level section parallel to the outlet of Huntley Pond. Some people may find this stretch to be frustrating for two reasons. First, one might clearly hear water tumbling loudly over a hidden cascade to the north of the stream—and on the wrong side of a private land boundary, clearly marked by the Northwoods Club. Second, the wide trail is plagued with mud. On what should be a brisk, easy section, you may be spending too much time watching your footing.

The trail cuts a corner through the club's property but then begins to climb out of the valley. The ascent is insignificant, but it does put the mud behind you. The final third of the trail is quite dry, actually, as it skirts the hills north of the river. Slowly you begin to hear the roar of the mighty Hudson, and tall white pines dot the woods. The trail scoots across some rocky patches and dips through a few draws before beginning its final descent. By the time you reach the brushy area immediately above the river, you have descended about 275 feet.

Upon arrival most people turn right, toward the upstream bend on the river. There is a moderate "beach" of sand nestled between the

Hudson Gorge raft. *Photo courtesy of the author*

boulders, and here is the best view of the eponymous cliffs. If you are here to watch the whitewater rafters and kayakers, this is where you'll get your first peek.

To the left of the trail's end you'll find a larger beach, then a path leading downstream to the camping area, located just above the point where the gorge pinches and the rapids resume. The site actually has multiple "rooms," and the whole arrangement seems big enough to accommodate a dozen tents—but remember, even here in the depths of the gorge, group-size regulations still apply.

The one downside to a trail that leads down into a gorge is that the hike back to your car will be mostly uphill. The climb is never steep, but if you were feeling better than expected as you hiked *down* to Blue Ledge, reality might catch up with you on the return *up* to Huntley Pond, regaining all that lost elevation.

16 Cascade Lake

Synopsis: Easy weekend camping trip at the site of an abandoned summer camp
Hiking Distance: 1.8 miles to first campsite
Elevation Change: Rolling terrain

I've previously described two overnight hikes in the Pigeon Lake Wilderness elsewhere in this guide, so pardon the indulgence as I add one more to the list. Cascade Lake near Eagle Bay probably needs little introduction for many people, since it's a rare weekend when I drive past the trailhead but see no cars parked here. Most of those people are day hikers, however, and few people seem to equate Cascade with backpacking. And yet a string of campsites along the north shore are very much worth noting.

At just over a mile long, Cascade Lake is one of the larger water bodies in the Forest Preserve requiring such a light effort to reach. It is a favorite family hike, and it is also a destination for a nearby outfitter offering horseback rides. Perhaps because it is so obvious, and not terribly remote, it gets overlooked by backpackers.

I have stayed at all three sites and have varying opinions of each. The swimming is good at Cascade, and this alone leads me to recommend this as a summer trip. However, not all of the sites would be equally enjoyable in all weather conditions; therefore, anyone coming here with a full backpack will have some choices to make.

Although an integral part of the Pigeon Lake Wilderness, this lake has its own history—which you can't help but notice as you explore the place. Rather than an old-growth forest, this tract once served time as a girls' camp many years ago. The buildings are all gone, of course, but traces are abundant in the vicinity of the campsites; it's rare as a guidebook writer that I get to refer to an old tennis court as a helpful aid in finding a wilderness campsite, but that's exactly what happens here. Even the trail itself is a relic; part of it was the main access road, and the rest was a bridle path.

There is one recent development worth noting. Although I've never encountered them here, the Department of Environmental

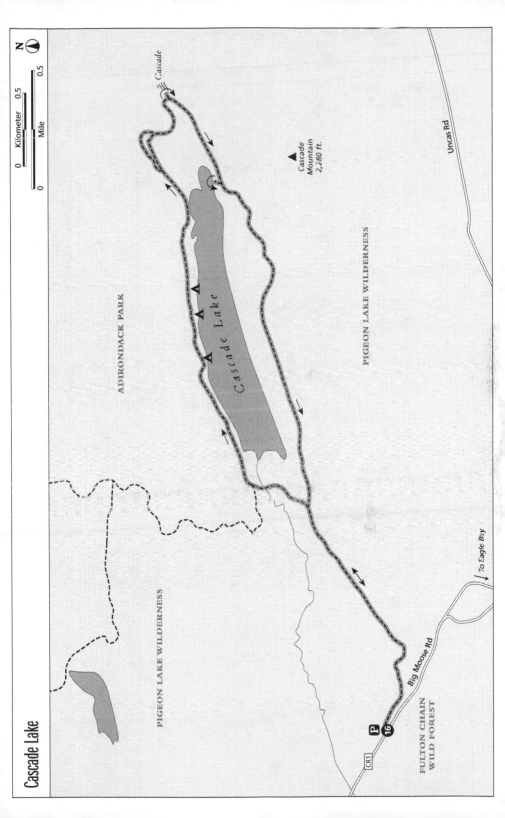

Cascade Lake

N

Kilometer 0.5

Mile 0.5

Cascade

Cascade Lake

Cascade
Mountain
2,280 ft.

ADIRONDACK PARK

PIGEON LAKE WILDERNESS

PIGEON LAKE WILDERNESS

FULTON CHAIN
WILD FOREST

Big Moose Rd

Uncas Rd

To Eagle Bay

CR1

P

16

Conservation has begun posting notices at the trailheads that ticks may be found at Cascade.

Getting There

Follow NY 28 to the hamlet of Eagle Bay, located near the Herkimer-Hamilton county line at Fourth Lake. From there, Big Moose Road leads northwest out of town and into state land. There are multiple trailhead parking areas (some of which have been described elsewhere in this guidebook), but for this recommended hike, stop at the Cascade Lake Trailhead on the right side of the road, 1.3 miles from Eagle Bay.

The Trail

From the parking area, the marked trail begins essentially as a connector that parallels Big Moose Road for the first 0.3 miles. It winds gently upward but descends sharply to a junction, where you turn hard left at the bottom of the slope. (The way right leads to the old trailhead, which was closed due to traffic safety concerns.)

Turning left, you are now following the obvious bed of an old road—in other words, the original access road to the camp—as it descends gently beneath the slopes of Cascade Mountain. At 1 mile you reach the junction where the loop trail around the lake comes in on the right. (More on that later.)

The main road curves down to the left and passes two clearings on the right, site of the old camp headquarters. Then you come to the lake's outlet, which you cross on a small bridge with intriguing wetland views both upstream and down.

Soon you reach a junction at 1.3 miles with a connecting trail to Queer Lake, but the old road leading straight ahead is both obvious and irresistible. Soon you get your first glimpses of the lake on your right, and at 1.8 miles the trail drops slightly to a prominent pine-shaded meadow.

This is not only a prime stopping point for day hikers, but also the meadow is the location of the first (and most prominent) campsite. This one has few equals in the Adirondacks; it is essentially a sprawling lawn kept in shadow by the towering trees, more parklike than any other

Cascade Lake campsite. *Photo courtesy of the author*

campsite in this book. Water access is great, and there is a privy nearby as well. The downside: when I stayed here, the entire campsite smelled like horse. Indeed, this site is a prime stop on the horseback riding tour.

The other two campsites are less obvious from the trail, perhaps because so few people seem curious enough to seek them out. The second site is just 0.2 miles beyond the horse meadow (2 miles total from the trailhead), about 100 feet off the trail to the right. The only clue might be the faint herd path leading out into a cleared area on the shoreline. This is perhaps the most stunning site, maybe even the best for swimming. However, unlike almost every other Adirondack campsite, this one has no shade. I stayed here on an August weekend that was warm but partly overcast—great for swimming, but had the sun been out this site would've been stifling hot.

The third site is another 0.1 miles down the main trail, or 2.1 miles from the parking area. It is also the least easy to find. As you pass through the foundations of the old summer camp, watch for odd patches of asphalt poking through the unnatural flatness to the right of the trail.

These are the remains of the tennis court, and the herd path down the bank to the third campsite turns right just beyond. This too is about 100 feet off the trail, but this one is much shadier and more screened from view.

The Cascade

Any visit to Cascade Lake invariably includes a visit to its namesake waterfall, located to the east of the lake. The continuing trail, of course, takes you right to it.

The trail narrows considerably as it makes its one close approach to the shoreline, way at the far east end of the lake. A few minutes later you will need to watch closely for the marked detour that veers left off the old bridle trail. The original route continued straight, sticking to the old roadway, but it was abandoned some years ago due to boggy conditions. The red-marked detour is a narrow footpath that hugs the hillside and crosses a footbridge before rejoining the bridle path in a spruce-and-balsam forest.

At 3.1 miles you reach an open area with a bridge across another inlet. Just out of sight up the inlet, to the left, is the cascade. Always a pretty sight, the unnamed stream falls 25 feet or so into a shallow splash pool, around which day hikers frequently pause.

The Loop around the Lake

The trail does not stop at the cascade but continues on a long loop around the lake. It begins to swing back westward immediately after passing the cascade, offering a so-so view of the lake at 3.5 miles. Otherwise the southern half of the loop is less scenic than the northern half as the trail winds right and left between Cascade Mountain and the ever-more-distant shoreline. Still, it is not an unpleasant hike, and at 4.9 miles the loop closes when you reconnect with the original trail.

Left leads in 1 mile back to the trailhead, and right leads in 0.8 miles back to the horse meadow campsite.

17 East Pond

Synopsis: Enjoy a remote campsite at the end of a low-maintenance trail
Hiking Distance: 4.3 miles
Elevation Change: Rolling terrain

The public lands comprising today's Ha-de-ron-dah Wilderness near Old Forge were assembled from the charred remains of a 1903 forest fire. Of the many blazes that afflicted the Adirondacks that year, this one was blamed on the sparks emitted from a passing locomotive; by the time the last flame sputtered out, some 20,000 acres or so of forest had been destroyed.

Previously this land had been designated "Wilderness Park," a private reserve owned by Julia Lyon deCamp, a member of a prominent landowning family in the southwestern Adirondacks. The area was said to be "well timbered" and was known in nineteenth-century guidebooks as the home to a scattered collection of trout ponds, each of them reached only by trail. But by 1909 deCamp's son and heir sold the land to the state, its timber value having literally gone up in smoke.

Conditions are now much better more than a century later, although people skilled at "reading" forests will certainly sense the extent of the fire as they pass through. The heart of today's Ha-de-ron-dah is a second-growth forest of fast-growing hardwoods—mature specimens of the same trees that, as seedlings, rushed into the cleared areas to soak in the sunshine. Prime among them are towering black cherry trees, which otherwise would've not grown in such populous numbers if the forest had remained deep, shady, and "primeval."

The name "Ha-de-ron-dah" is a pseudo-word of purported Iroquois origin. According to received wisdom it means "bark eater," although I've not been able to confirm its authenticity. (The closest I found was the Mohawk phrase *ron de ron deh*, which I'm told means the same thing but is pronounced "lon de loon deh.")

Regardless, the term *bark eater* refers to the foundational story of the Adirondacks and the era preceding its written history. The story tells of the warring Iroquois and Algonquin nations that frequently

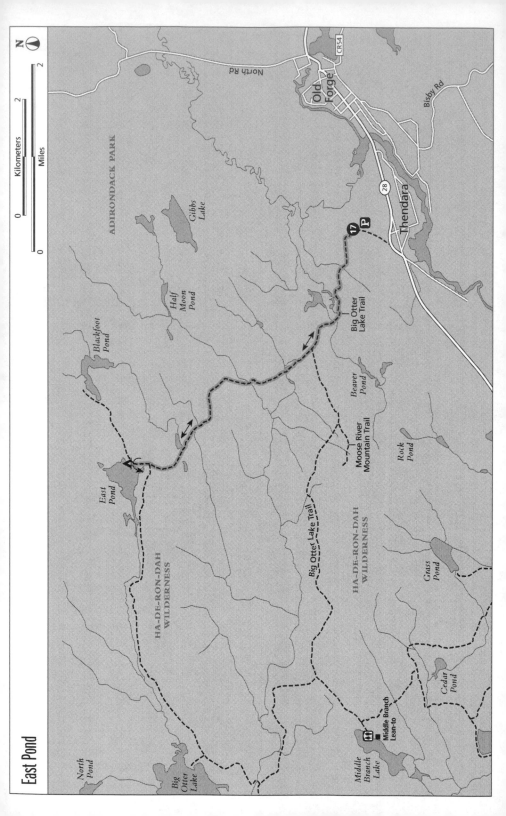

East Pond

encountered and taunted each other here, including one legendary instance when one of the two peoples observed members of the other reduced to eating bark in a desperate bid for survival. The details of who was taunting who varies on each retelling, but nevertheless "Adirondack" is presumed to be an English-language corruption of "Ha-de-ron-dah". . . . which, if true, leads to the interesting conclusion that the name of our beautiful park is derived from a pre-Columbian put-down.

East Pond is located in the northern half of the Ha-de-ron-dah Wilderness, at the head of the eastern tributary to nearby Big Otter Lake. It is a beautiful spot that goes unseen by most people, partly because the trails leading to it are intentionally placed on a minimal-maintenance rotation by the Department of Environmental Conservation to retain the area's rugged appearance. Beyond a certain point on this hike, the trails appear lightly used and may go through cycles of neglect, but if you understand this is the normal condition at East Pond and accept the challenge, you will be treated to a rare solitary adventure in a region that is otherwise astir with tourist activity.

Getting There

The trailhead is located on the periphery of Thendara, the companion hamlet to Old Forge. Follow NY 28 south from the center of town to the railroad overpass, and then turn north onto Herreshoff Road. This unpaved road parallels the train tracks and ends at a gate 0.4 miles from the highway, with plenty of room to park off to the side.

The Trail

This humble parking area at the beginning of a gated road with derelict railcars nearby may seem like an inauspicious start to a wilderness hike, but things quickly improve as you walk past the gate. Within 250 feet signs point left for the trail to state land, and soon the route enters the woods and reaches the state land boundary at 0.4 miles.

The trail descends in stages to the wetlands surrounding Indian Brook, which you cross at around 1 mile. Then you pass through a piece of the cherry-filled forest en route to a junction with the side trail to East Pond at 1.5 miles.

East Pond. *Photo courtesy of the author*

The "minimal maintenance" section begins here as you make the right turn to the northwest. In just 0.3 miles (1.8 miles total), you reach the sprawling wetlands at South Inlet, which has long been a major problem for this trail. For many years, hikers have had to take their chances crossing one of the soggy beaver dams, grappling with the alders in their way to maintain balance, due to the lack of any better alternatives. In 2023, however, work crews installed a new log bridge that should hopefully make this crossing a nonissue for at least a few years to come.

As the trail rises away from the beaver flows, it spends time in a hardwood forest with a wide-open understory, where the track has sometimes been faintly defined on the ground. At 2.6 miles you cross another stream on whatever rocks are available and then angle more westerly through the deep forest.

More wetlands are encountered at 3.2 miles, followed by an intriguing area a few minutes later, at 3.5 miles. Here the woods beside the trail are the thickest you've seen all day, the result of a 1988 tornado that touched down near Little Simon Pond, cleared a patch of forest, and thus instigated the vigorous new growth seen today. The trail is clear, but the thick woods discourage people from straying upstream to explore Little Simon. Instead, you cross the stream in a rugged little rock flume and then observe the pond as the trail skirts past its west end.

The 1903 forest fire reached its northern limit in this vicinity, and as you proceed over the next hill there is indeed a corresponding improvement in the forest quality. The trail ascends 140 feet over a hill and then gives back most of that elevation as it descends to the north.

At 4 miles you reach a trail intersection near the southeastern corner of East Pond. Keep right, drawing closer to the pond. The side trail to Blackfoot Pond bears right at 4.2 miles, but if you keep left you'll cross a small stream and reach the sole designated campsite on East Pond, 4.3 miles from the trailhead.

The campsite is set back from the water but is otherwise well situated on high, level ground surrounded by hardwood forests. The continuing trail leads past the site of a long-gone lean-to (which many people now have a hard time finding, the traces are so faint) toward the tip of a prominent peninsula on the pond's east shore. The views here are lined up well with the long western arm, with piney islets nearby.

PART III
CANOE CAMPING

The Adirondacks are more than a mountain range. This is also a region of lakes and rivers, coming in a wide variety of sizes and personalities. Take tiny little Lake Tear of the Clouds, for instance: a tarn just below Mount Marcy's summit, noteworthy for being the highest pond in the Hudson River watershed. No one would cart a canoe *there* except to stubbornly prove a point. But just a few miles away is Henderson Lake, an outstanding waterbody nestled at the foot of the same group of mountains—a place that absolutely *should* be paddled.

Paddling in the Adirondacks opens up an entirely new realm of exploration. Many of the campsites described in the previous chapters extolled the delights of camping *next* to a remote body of water, but in most cases you will spend your visits there gazing out across the water wondering what lies around those distant bends in the shoreline. With a canoe or kayak available, you can go see.

There are thousands of lakes in the Adirondacks, and paddling can occur anywhere there is direct public access to the water. However, the routes that attract me to them most—and the ones that I've included in part III—are those that lead away from civilization in the shortest distance possible. If I am going to paddle for several miles to some distant point, perhaps facing a headwind in the process, I want to spend the night someplace worthy of the effort.

Unlike hiking trails—narrow, predefined routes with known destinations—an open waterway presents nearly infinite possibilities. No two paddlers will ever follow the same route from one end of a lake to the other. And in terms of remote campsites, the options will be arrayed across miles of shoreline—here an island, there a promontory, and way over there a secluded beach. These places invite continuous

Cage Lake Springhole lean-to. *Photo courtesy of the author*

reexploration; you can stay at a different site each time you return—an experience not unlike working through the menu of your favorite restaurant, one dinner at a time.

Each selection describes a paddling route leading to multiple campsites—dozens in some cases. Some, like Little Tupper Lake, may require strenuous paddling against a stiff headwind. Others, like Lake Lila, may require a carry between the parking area and the nearest point on the shoreline. A few, like the Cedar River Flow, may also be open to motorboats. Each one, however, provides a unique experience that would be difficult to replicate elsewhere.

18　Little Tupper Lake

Synopsis: Paddle a large lake with rock ledges, small islands, private beaches, and a dash of history

Paddling Distance: 1 to 4.5 miles

Number of Campsites: 24

Little Tupper Lake is only "little" when directly compared to its namesake, "Big" Tupper Lake just up the road. It is actually about 5.5 miles in length and anywhere from 0.5 to 1 mile in width, making this among the larger lakes in the Forest Preserve—and the largest Adirondack waterbody on which the public use of motors is prohibited.

Its temperament, however, is often determined by the weather. Many of my early visits to Little Tupper seemed to overlap with days that began perfectly calm but later became marred by surly wind gusts. This resulted in afternoons filled with choppy waters that were unpleasant (to say the least) for paddling.

These experiences instilled in me a healthy respect for the lake. Eventually I learned to avoid coming on breezy days, or to at least get off the water when the wind started, and that's when I discovered Little Tupper can actually be a peaceful place when its surface isn't being roiled into canoe-tipping whitecaps. And, waves or not, traversing the lake is far less of an ordeal without a headwind pushing against you.

For many years, the lake was the gem of a large private reserve owned by the heirs of William C. Whitney, a demigod of the Gilded Age who in the spirit of his times dabbled in both business and politics. Whitney Park was primarily a timber investment, but as the property was passed from heir to heir, the urgency to liquidate the cash value of its forests only seemed to increase. By 1997, when New York State successfully negotiated the lake's purchase from Marylou Whitney, most of the acreage surrounding its shores had been high-graded—meaning every tree of value had been harvested, leaving behind a scraggly growth of saplings and beleaguered seed trees. Whitney Park had become the butt of local jokes: a woodpecker entering the place had to carry a lunch pail.

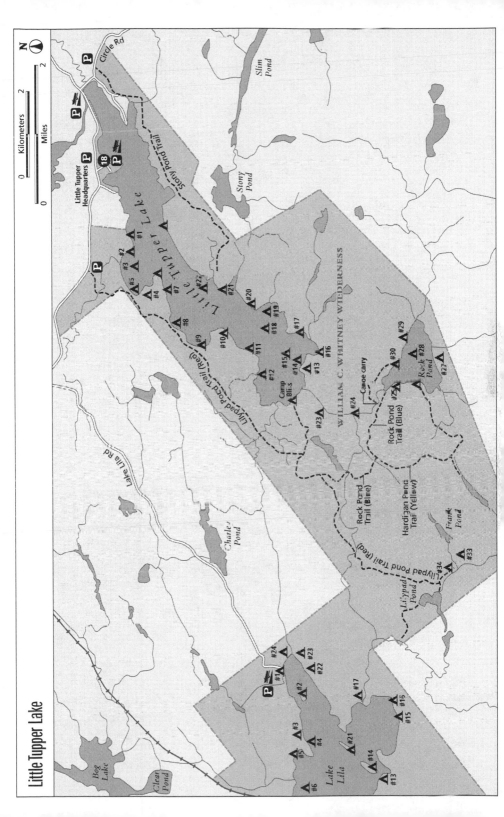

Little Tupper Lake

Since 2000, however, the lake has been managed as the eastern entrance to the William C. Whitney Wilderness—one of the park's smaller protected areas, but just the right size for weekend paddling adventures. Eschewed by many people as a hiking destination because of the logging history (although that situation has greatly improved since June 1998, when it opened to the public), Whitney excels as a *paradis des pagayeurs*, or "paddler's paradise." The lake offers a wide variety of campsites, from islands to promontories to beaches, and few impacts from all of the former logging activities are evident from the water.

Getting There

Little Tupper Lake is one of a cluster of paddling destinations located to the west of NY 30, the primary highway between the villages of Long Lake and Tupper Lake. The key to finding them is Sabattis Road, which turns west from the highway 7.1 miles north of Long Lake or 11.5 miles south of Tupper Lake. At a three-way intersection at Little Tupper's outlet, continue west for another 1.3 miles to Little Tupper Headquarters, a facility that serves as a ranger station, employee housing, and a public canoe launch. Brown Department of Environmental Conservation signs mark all of the turns from NY 30; therefore, the parking area should not be hard to find despite being 4.2 miles from the highway.

The Lake

The parking area is set back from the water by about 150 feet, mandating a short but easy carry to launch your boat and get under way. Little Tupper trends on a gentle arc from northeast to southwest, with three large bays indenting its northern shore. Aside from the Headquarters facility, there are two remaining private camps to the east and west, but in my experience, these are seldom occupied and can be easily forgotten with distance.

There are 24 designated campsites on this lake, the nearest located about a mile west of the canoe launch. The rest are well spaced around the shoreline and on five of the islands—and all but a very small number of them are quite good.

The southern shoreline is the most rugged, in that it tends toward rockiness and has almost no beaches. One mile-long stretch is essentially the foot of a hill with no campsites at all. But this side of the lake also has the richest bounty of islands, most of which tend to be somewhat small and delightful. A few of the mainland campsites are not particularly noteworthy, but they do provide good jumping-off points for some of the interior ponds included in the 1997 acquisition, particularly Antediluvian Pond with its quaint pre-Darwinian name.

By contrast, the north side of the lake seems to have been sculpted during the declining days of the last Ice Age. The mainland repeatedly advances and retreats in a series of bogs and bays, resulting in a more diverse array of camping options. Yes, there are rock promontories aplenty, as well as an island campsite in the northernmost bay, but several campsites near the southern end of the lake come with "private" sand beaches. The best of these are capped with artistic stands of red pine trees.

There is also a spot of history at site #7, known as Regan Point, where paddlers following the northern shoreline will notice a chimney standing behind a pair of pylons rising out of the water. This was the site of a camp built by one of the more engineering-minded members of the Whitney clan, who placed a giant cistern on high ground back in the woods to fuel a gravity-fed plumbing system. The buildings are gone, but a second chimney remains not far from the first. Curious campers can still find the cistern, parts of the plumbing network, masonry remnants, and a second set of pylons in a nearby cove where a boathouse once stood.

Note that the adventures do no stop at Little Tupper. Paddlers can continue past the lake through a 1.5-mile-long, beaver-dammed stream channel to Rock Pond, one of the epitomes of remote paddling in the Adirondacks. This destination can be reached in a day, making it technically "doable" as a one-night camping trip, but it pains me to think of Rock that way. A lake this big and this far into the woods deserves a longer visit, and while I've seen people sojourning there for a single night, their visits were so pitifully brief I can't imagine what they had the time to see.

Little Tupper Lake. *Photo courtesy of the author*

Little Tupper Lake is the source of a heritage strain of brook trout, and for that reason all trout fishing here is catch-and-release only. Loons thrive on these waters, and their nighttime vocal performances may be among the best you'll hear in the Adirondacks.

Blackfly populations can be vexing in the early season, although a steady breeze may provide some remedy. When the lake is calm its length can be paddled in a couple hours, but headwinds can add significant time and effort to your voyage.

19 Round Lake

Synopsis: The smaller neighbor to Little Tupper Lake, right-sized for weekend canoe camping
Paddling Distance: 1.2 to 2.8 miles
Number of Campsites: 11

Not only is Round Lake physically attached to Little Tupper by a long, continuous channel of water, but the two share a similar history. The area north of Sabattis Road was also once part of Whitney Park and was an essential part of early logging operations. However, before the high-grading that "liquidated" much of Little Tupper's forest took place, the heirs of William C. Whitney sold this northern acreage to International Paper, one of the largest landowners in the Adirondacks at the time. The land was certainly "used" prior to the state's acquisition in 2006, but more gently so.

Today, Round Lake is the centerpiece of the Round Lake Wilderness—the second-smallest protected area in the park, but still plenty big enough to serve up quality outdoor adventures. It shares many qualities with nearby Little Tupper, although this lake is substantially shorter and never quite achieves the full sense of remoteness as its larger sibling. Rather, this is a perfectly fine lake for a relatively easy two-day camping trip, allowing paddlers to set off and return without a huge investment in time.

Getting There

Round Lake is one of a cluster of paddling destinations located to the west of NY 30, the primary highway between the villages of Long Lake and Tupper Lake. The key to finding them is Sabattis Road, which turns west from the highway 7.1 miles north of Long Lake or 11.5 miles south of Tupper Lake. At a three-way intersection at Little Tupper's outlet, turn west. The small parking area for Round Lake is reached immediately on the right, about 2.9 miles from the highway. Brown Department of Environmental Conservation signs mark all of the turns from NY 30, making this spot relatively easy to find.

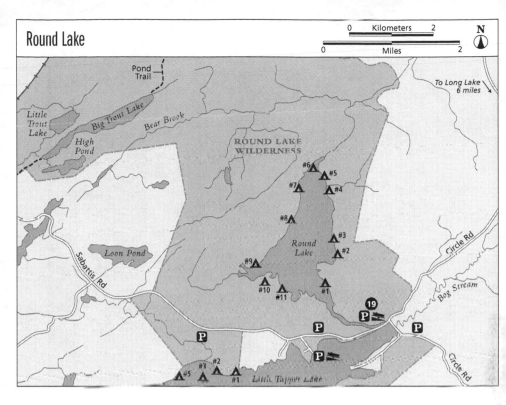

The Lake

No significant carries are required to reach Round Lake, just a short drop down the road berm to the water. However, there is about a mile of delayed gratification as you paddle the umbilical channel connecting the two lakes. The waterway slowly widens and the boggy shorelines part, revealing the main body of the lake.

It doesn't take a geometry whiz to see Round Lake is not round in shape. Its name is a common peculiarity in the Adirondacks, where none of the so-named lakes are anything close to being circular. Rather, "round" is probably a reference to the round whitefish, *Prosopium cylindraceum*, a once-common fish with a tubular body that is now considered endangered in New York State.

The lake is more deltoid than round, with its two longest sides tapering to a point at its northernmost tip. Paddlers arriving from Sabattis Road enter at the southeastern corner of the triangle, and in good weather it should only take about an hour to span the full length of the lake.

Round Lake Dam. *Photo courtesy of the author*

More than half of the lake's 11 campsites can be found on the east shore, and several of these had been private cabin sites prior to public acquisition. The remaining sites on the west shore tend to be more rugged and isolated. None are located on islands because Round has no islands big enough for camping. However, the best (and most coveted) sites on the east shore will come with small sand beaches.

One historic curiosity remains. If you paddle all the way up to the outlet at the north end of the lake, you will find a low concrete dam raising the water by a modest amount. This structure is a relic from the early Whitney timber harvests, when spruce logs were floated by stream to "Big" Tupper Lake—an operation that was replaced in the 1930s by a short-lived spur railroad to the south, near Rock Pond. A carry trail extends northeast along the east bank of Round Lake Stream, the first mile of which is one of the best streamside hikes in the Adirondacks. This small river performs a series of dramatic drops from one flume to the next, and in a few places it is still possible to find rock berms built by the lumbermen in a bid to straighten the channel.

20　Lake Lila

Synopsis: A highly popular lake with a nearby hiking trail, numerous sand beaches, and several islands
Paddling Distance: 0.3-mile canoe carry, with campsites appearing from 0 to 2.6 miles once on the water
Number of Campsites: 24, including one lean-to

If you were to read the driving directions to Lake Lila prior to learning any other detail, you might draw the reasonable conclusion that this is an obscure location with little recreational usage. Nothing about the long, bumpy drive to the public parking area, or the short-but-tiring canoe carry to the shore, would lead anyone unfamiliar with the area to suspect this was a popular canoe-camping destination.

And yet all of Lake Lila's secrets were discovered long ago. Indeed, this is often regarded as a popular destination, and in the summer the carry trail connecting the parking area to the lake is one of the busiest trails anywhere in Adirondack Park. The attraction is not just the largest lake wholly within the Forest Preserve but also one of the prettiest, with numerous wild sand beaches, four substantial islands, and two dozen prime camping spots.

Lila anchors the western end of the William C. Whitney Wilderness, not far from where it shares a common boundary with the Five Ponds Wilderness. At 1,409 acres in size, it is quite large from a paddler's perspective and comes with some of the wind-driven hazards frequently associated with Little Tupper Lake, including the possibility of whitecaps. Still, the beauties are irresistible, and so the people come.

The lake's history is comparable to that of Little Tupper and Round: once part of a large private estate, it opened to the public in a landmark acquisition. In this case the land was owned by William Seward Webb, a regional railroad baron. Determined to open a new rail line through the western Adirondacks, but unable to convince the state to grant him a right-of-way, Webb leveraged his wealth to purchase vast sums of land and forge his own corridor. The line was completed in 1892.

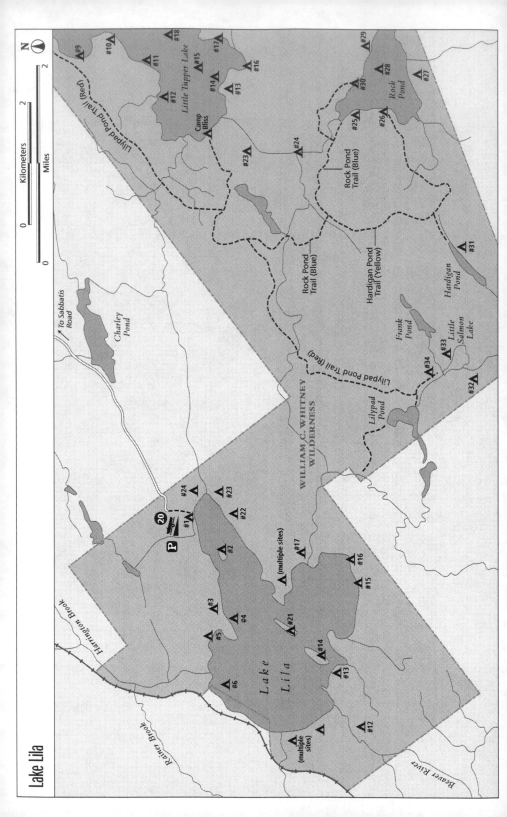

Lake Lila

Webb was so impressed with one of his acquisitions that he renamed it after his wife, Lila Osgood Vanderbilt, and built a lodge on its west shore. In its heyday, Nehasane Park (pronounced "ne-HASS-any") incorporated some 115,000 acres throughout the headwaters of the Beaver River, bounding the equally impressive Whitney and Brandreth Parks to the east and south. His lodge was serviced by its own rail station located at the foot of nearby Frederica Mountain, named for his daughter.

New York State acquired 14,600 acres from Webb's heirs in 1978, more than fifty years after his death. This included the entirety of Lake Lila, part of Shingle Shanty Brook, and a string of mountains to the west. The lake's renaissance as a public paddling destination began at this time, and its reputation has not dimmed since.

Getting There

Lake Lila is one of a cluster of paddling destinations located to the west of NY 30, the primary highway between the villages of Long Lake and Tupper Lake. The key to finding them is Sabattis Road, which turns west from the highway 7.1 miles north of Long Lake or 11.5 miles south of Tupper Lake. At a three-way intersection at Little Tupper's outlet, continue west for another 4.5 miles to the start of the Lake Lila Access Road, a left turn.

This access road is 5.6 miles long, all of it narrow and bumpy, though otherwise passable by ordinary automobiles. However, it is gated every year from December through mid-May. In the summer and fall, parking is confined to a spacious parking area that can nevertheless fill up on some peak weekends; no parking is allowed along the road.

Brown Department of Environmental Conservation signs mark all of the turns from NY 30; therefore, the parking area should not be hard to find despite being 13 miles from the highway.

The Lake

The canoe carry begins on the south side of the parking area and leads for 0.3 miles down to a beach at the eastern tip of the lake; how often you need to use it depends on how efficiently you can shuttle your canoe and all of your gear down to the water. Once there, however, the camping opportunities begin immediately, with one accessible directly from the trail—without the need to paddle anywhere.

This northeastern bay is good at funneling headwinds straight in your direction; therefore, in the wrong conditions your biggest challenge might be negotiating the 1.3 miles or so to the main body of the lake. There, two large islands may provide partial cover from the wind.

In terms of campsites, they are literally found in every direction, including one "stray" site tucked partway down the outlet. There are four island sites and numerous others with private sand beaches or scenic rock ledges—very few sites at Lake Lila might be categorized as "unpleasant." If you are the lucky paddler who has the pick of the lot, with no one else around, then you first need to ask what you prefer most: seclusion, community, or easy access.

The most secluded sites are those found on the distant southern shoreline, each of them easily more than 2 miles from the carry trail. The two largest islands, Spruce and Buck, may also fall into this category. By contrast, there are "campsite clusters" on the eastern and western shores where the sounds of voices may carry across the water if all the sites are in use at the same time.

The other factor that campers should consider is the private access road that hugs the northern and eastern shorelines, which is still used sporadically by landowners to the west to reach Partlow and Nehasane Lakes. And the railroad is expected to see an increase in usage as tourist service resumes between Old Forge and Tupper Lake. Some campers may not notice (or may even appreciate) these sounds, but people in search of a "get away from it all" experience might find the sense of wilderness remoteness somewhat lacking all along the northwest quadrant of the lake.

Any visit to Lake Lila would be incomplete without a hike up Frederica Mountain. There is a trailhead landing on the west shore, a short distance north of the former site of Nehasane Lodge, with trail signs guiding you along the 1.5-mile route. It begins by following the private road to Partlow Lake, crossing the refurbished railroad tracks, and then veering right onto a foot trail that climbs 460 feet to the summit. The best views—and by "best" I mean *gorgeous*—can be found from a rock ledge below and to the left of the trail's terminus.

Beach landing at Lake Lila. *Photo courtesy of the author*

There are peripheral channels to explore as well, including Shingle Shanty Brook to the east and a short section of the Beaver River to the southwest. In both cases, public access ends at the private land boundaries, which you can expect will be well marked.

21 Cedar River Flow

Synopsis: A marshy lake with outstanding mountain views
Paddling Distance: 0.5 to 4 miles
Number of Campsites: 8, including one lean-to

Among my first loves is the Cedar River Flow, an artificial lake with abundant wildlife and outstanding mountain views. I "discovered" this place early in my canoe-camping career and have held a soft spot for it ever since. The ever-changing views, as well as the wild surprises sometimes concealed in the rushes that dominate the southern half of the lake, conspire to make this a superb paddling destination.

About 75 percent of the shoreline is part of the West Canada Lake Wilderness, although the lake itself is not. This technicality allows motorboats to share these waters, although the rustic condition of the boat launch and the marshy nature of much of the lake help keep the boat sizes small.

As portrayed on maps, the Cedar River Flow is about 3 miles long. However, only the northern half of the flow might be realistically called a "lake," with the southernmost mile better resembling a marsh—and the deeper you penetrate that marsh, the thicker the vegetation gets. Eventually even canoes become restricted to the main channels, and very few motors make it as far as the Cedar River itself.

The Cedar River flows in from the south, and the first mile or so (once you find the entrance) is easily navigable, as far as the carry lean-to. From this point, people looking to stretch their legs with a few trail miles can link up with the Northville-Placid Trail and explore farther up the Cedar River valley.

Getting There

Wakely Dam, where this adventure starts, is a long way from the nearest main highway, but in the summer this byway is frequently traveled. Beginning in downtown Indian Lake, follow NY 28/30 west out of town for 2.2 miles and turn left onto Cedar River Road. This begins as

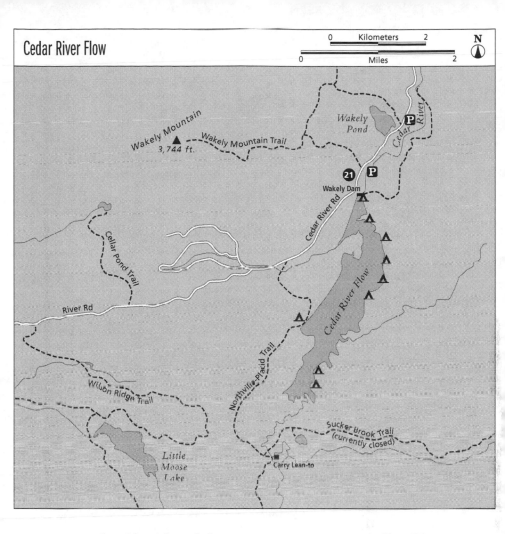

a paved residential road that never seems to cease winding. The pavement ends at about 7.8 miles, but the road pushes ahead into the ever-deepening woods. You pass scenic Wakely Pond at 11 miles, and then arrive at the large clearing known as Wakely Dam 12.1 miles from the state highway.

Wakely Dam is itself a campground, popular among RV owners. The sites here are free and available on a first-come basis, but they come with few amenities other than a handful of privies. The canoe launch is located just before the dam, with a parking area crudely defined in the middle of the clearing.

The Lake

Your paddle trip begins just above the dam, in a small bay that doesn't live up to the scenic promise of the main lake. This bay is offset a few degrees west of the flow's central axis; therefore, the first order of business is to round the corner. A few small islands stand guard over the connecting channel, and as you veer south again, several of the region's largest mountains start coming into view.

Headwinds commonly blow in from the south here, and you may find yourself suddenly exposed. Of the eight campsites located on the lake, all but one are found on the east shore. There are mountains in every direction: Buck and Buell to the east, Payne and Wakely to the northwest, Little Moose and Manbury to the southwest. My personal favorite is the striking profile of Blue Ridge Mountain several miles due south of the flow, identified by its rock scars.

A few of the east shore campsites are unusual in their proximity to the water. During one early visit I fretted that I was squatting illegally in the canoe landing, and that the true campsite had to be somewhere deeper inland. But no, these are the campsites! On another visit, I once had to pass one of these same sites by when I found it temporarily occupied by a family of Canada geese.

Other sites are notable for the preponderance of paper birch trees found in the surrounding woods. This pleasing (and useful) tree species is particularly common throughout this region, and its flammable bark is a favorite source of kindling. Feel free to take part in this tradition, with the caveat that campers should only be using those pieces already discarded by the tree. Birch bark found on the ground is fair game; birch bark still attached to the tree, however loosely, is still part of a living organism. You will probably find many barkless birch trees in close proximity to the more popular campsites, stripped bare by overeager sports who failed to heed this advice.

As you paddle past the mouth of Buell Brook, the lake becomes shallower and more marshlike. Beginning in June, rushes and reeds start growing thicker, providing cover for all manner of waterfowl, as well as the occasional antlered megafauna. (I've never seen moose here, but I've heard reports. And this lake seems like it should be right up a moose's

Cedar River Flow. *Photo courtesy of the author*

alley.) Among the more distinctive plants are the bur-reeds, which surely must have been the inspiration for the brutal medieval mace.

Proceeding south, you will become more reliant on the open channels, which seem to preserve the bends of the original river from the days before the dam; paddling off-course becomes increasingly difficult thanks to the emergent vegetation. But the channels will also helpfully guide you to the mouth of the Cedar River, which quickly leads you into a whole new realm.

Paddling upstream, you begin in a bed of alders with very little solid ground within reach. But gradually regular banks do emerge, including one sandy specimen with a well-used campsite perched atop it. Spruce-covered slopes come next, until about a mile above the flow you reach the carry lean-to, used frequently by both hikers and paddlers. It's epithet is "the lean-to that hums," which unfairly implies this spot is somehow buggier than the rest of the flow area. In truth, the blackflies and mosquitoes are evenly distributed, prepared to bestow misery upon any unprepared visitor who dares come calling during their respective peak seasons.

22 Oswegatchie River

Synopsis: The preeminent river for wilderness canoe camping in the Adirondacks
Paddling Distance: 1.8 to 10.7 miles
Number of Campsites: 34, including four lean-tos

While the word *Adirondack* conjures for many people images of mountains and crowded trails, the serenely enchanting Oswegatchie River and its floodplain is a landscape that resolves itself into gentle hills and winding streams. It might almost sound bucolic if it were not so essentially *wild*. Rather than the in-your-face scenery of a mountainous country, this place gets under your skin with its bird-rich wetlands, its sensuous and graceful pines, and a long list of little details that let you know you are no longer in an environment of man-made contrivances.

From Inlet Landing upstream to its source, the Oswegatchie is one long, sluggish channel with most of its elevation change located at one site, High Falls. Nearly all of it is navigable, even during the driest summer. The river has a few riffles, shallows, and shoals—some of which, for lack of the real thing and with perhaps a little humor—have been bestowed with the name *rapids*. Beaver dams and the occasional log are also encountered, but these are minor inconveniences between long stretches of flat, easy water.

What may prove to be greater impediments are the numerous channels and pseudo-channels that entwine the main course, often confusing your choice of route upstream. In low water, even trying to follow the strongest flow of water may prove difficult. In high water, you do have to contend with a good current.

It has long been a matter of speculation just how long the river really is. While it is easy to measure the straight-line distances between major landmarks on a map, for many years it was nearly impossible to measure the river's overlapping squiggles—the distance you actually paddle. It therefore seems sacrilegious to offer the following approximate measurements, which were determined by using modern mapping software. Not to fear, though, because the Oswegatchie will always retain the upper hand so long as it has the freedom to adjust its course over time.

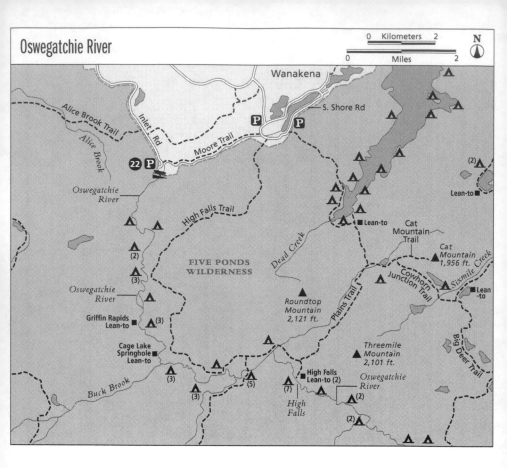

The river features four lean-tos and dozens of tent sites. Note that good drinking water is scarce, however. The river is so stained with natural tannins that standard filtering and purification methods may not remove all the impurities—or will age your filter prematurely. Canoe campers are advised to bring as much drinking water as they can carry.

Also, the river's tight oxbows, hairpin corners, and frequent beaver dams clearly favor canoes 16 feet or shorter with at least some rocker (i.e., an ability to turn without much fuss). Longer canoes, as well as kayaks, will be at a distinct disadvantage.

Getting There

All paddling access to the Oswegatchie River begins at the end of Inlet Road, which heads south from NY 3 from a point a mile east of the derelict Benson Mines, near the Clifton-Fine town line and the hamlet of Star Lake. It is a narrow gravel road that winds for 3.2 miles through the Forest Preserve to a secluded point at the Oswegatchie River known as Inlet Landing, a large grassy clearing with ample room for parking. At the peak of the summer canoeing season, this can be a busy place.

The River

The first 0.8-mile stretch of river above Inlet Landing is relatively wide and straight, with a handful of cedar trees (rare for this region) located on the right. The river then enters the first alder bed and begins to wind relentlessly. It takes about 45 minutes before you begin to pass the first of the river's designated campsites, indicated by numbered markers. Shortly after passing site #45, the river takes a brief break from its oxbows at a spot known as Straight of the Woods, about 2.3 river miles above Inlet Landing.

The river resumes its sinuous course at the next alder bed, and at 3.3 miles, or after about 90 minutes of paddling, you reach High Rock, which is a bluff that rises vertically out of the depths of the river. There is a scenic and very popular campsite (#41) located near the top, with a trail leading inland to the High Falls Loop Trail. It is worth stopping for the view of the river. People who know their Oswegatchie landmarks well can spot the location of the Griffin Rapids lean-to 0.9 miles farther upstream—as the white-throated sparrow flies. The river will take you there in 1.5 miles.

During that distance, the river is far from solid ground. The surrounding alders rise high above you, especially when the water is low, so most of your views are confined to your immediate surroundings. You reach the Griffin Rapids lean-to in just over two hours, at 4.8 miles. The "rapids" are merely a set of riffles where the rocky riverbed is briefly close to the surface. They seem quite innocuous, but it is sobering to remember that a paddler drowned a short distance upstream from here in 2003. The woods behind the lean-to were acquired at a tax sale in 1884; they were never logged.

Oswegatchie River. *Photo courtesy of the author*

The next section of river brings you closer to a boreal forest of white pine, tamaracks, spruce, and fir. The Cage Lake Springhole lean-to—a prized campsite under a stand of tall, straight pines—is another hour's paddle upstream, at 6.1 miles. This spot, or a tent site about 0.3

miles farther upstream, is highly recommended for birders. Buck Brook, which carries the combined contributions of Buck Pond, Cage Lake, and Hammer Creek, empties into the pool in front of the lean-to.

Upstream, the river's turns become tighter, its current quicker, and its obstacles sterner and less forgiving. Shortly, though, the river straightens itself out and becomes gentle again. Site #30 is Camp Betsy, once the haunt of old-time guide Wilfred Morrison. As you approach site #28, the former Rich Lumber Company's railroad grade pulls near the river on the left. This too is part of the High Falls Loop Trail. The submerged rocks and quickened current here comprise Ross Rapids; its small campsite is located between the rapids and the hiking trail, 7.9 miles from Inlet.

The forested bends that follow are among the river's prettiest. One shallow section, Straight Rapids, may require lining in the summer. A few turns after site #27, at 8.6 miles, you reach the mouth of Wolf Pond Outlet. Site #26 was once the location of the camp of Art Leary, another Wanakena guide notable for constructing the shortest trail to Five Ponds (which happened to pass right by his camp).

Allow two hours for the paddle upstream from Cage Lake Spring-hole to the footbridge that marks where the trail to Five Ponds and Wolf Pond departs, 9 miles above Inlet Landing. There is a large landing here on the right, with three designated campsites in the vicinity. The swift water under the bridge is Round Hill Rapids, which may not always be passable with a paddle. It is possible to carry through two of the campsites on the south bank if necessary. The uppermost site, #22, is located near a small spring that remains the best source of drinking water on the river.

The river remains reasonably straight for the next half mile as it passes through woods rich with large white pine. You reach Crooked Rapids, which will require lining in low water conditions, and then return to the alder beds at a place called Carter Landing. Glasby Creek flows in at 9.6 miles. The river turns tightly, with the sound of roaring water getting closer. Then, as it straightens out, High Falls appears at 10.7 miles.

There are landings on both sides of the river. On the right side is the more secluded western lean-to. The left landing is the canoe carry to the upper river, as well as the route to additional campsites and the eastern lean-to. The water drops no more than 15 feet over the falls, but considering the sluggish Oswegatchie, it is a remarkable sight! Do not expect solitude, though, especially on weekends. High Falls is one of the most popular backcountry destinations in the Five Ponds Wilderness, with some of the litter and erosion to show for it. One large campsite below the falls has been permanently closed by the Department of Environmental Conservation due to degraded conditions.

A set of concrete pillars above the falls invariably inspire much conjecture, but alas their origins are really quite banal. These are the remains of a footbridge that once connected the two lean-tos—removed many years ago to protect the wilderness aesthetic, even though the pylons were left behind.

High Falls is a worthy destination after a day's paddling, although many people find it difficult to paddle this entire distance in a single day—let alone continue past the falls to the remaining nine campsites upstream. Rather, consider this one a scalable adventure. Paddle up the Oswegatchie until you find an available campsite that suits your fancy, and when possible hop onto the High Falls Loop Trail to hike the remaining distance to the waterfall.

23 Garnet Lake

Synopsis: A secluded adventure where you least expect it
Paddling Distance: 0.3 to 1.2 miles
Number of Campsites: 6

Don't be put off by the fact that Garnet Lake, located near Crane Mountain in the Wilcox Lake Wild Forest, is a small man-made lake with dozens of camps along its north end. Once you round the corner of the lake and put all that behind you, this is an outstanding little body of water! There are six boat-access campsites along its shore, each one increasingly secluded as you paddle southward, but none is more than 1.2 miles from the canoe launch.

When Garnet was dammed circa 1853, it was called Mill Creek Lake. Lumber was its first industry, although garnets were discovered in a few nearby locations and mined in small operations around the turn of the twentieth century. The name change to Garnet Lake, though, appears to be an instance of rebranding, when guide Frank Maxam bought an 89-acre property on its south shore in 1905. He opened a rustic lodge here and named it the Garnet Lake Camp, and soon the lake's old name passed out of memory.

The lake is not large, and stumps from the original pre-dam forest make much of it inaccessible to motorboats. Canoes, on the other hand, are far less fragile in this regard. The 302-acre lake sits in a basin surrounded by hills and mountains on nearly all sides; if you are looking for a place to spend the night, your site selection process will largely hinge upon your preferred view.

Getting There

The easiest way to find Garnet Lake is to take NY 8 to the hamlet of Johnsburg, between Bakers Mills and Wevertown. There, turn southwest onto Garnet Lake Road and follow it into the Mill Creek valley—enjoying the outstanding views of Crane Mountain along the way. Look for the right (west) turn at 6.3 miles, where a second

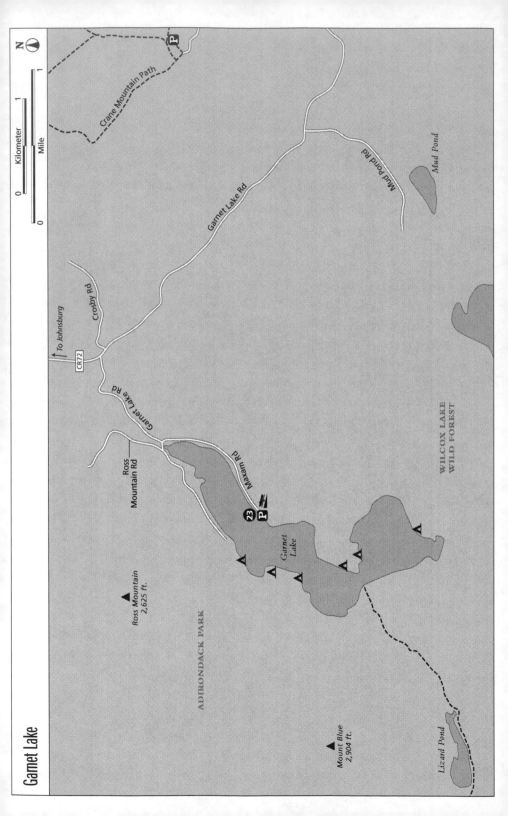

Garnet Lake. *Photo oourtcsy of the aulhui*

road—which signs label Garnet Lake Road as well, although it has gone by the name Maxam Road in the past—leads uphill and out of the valley. Follow it for 0.7 miles and bear left at the junction near the outlet; the public parking area is located 0.8 miles farther, at the end of the town road.

The Lake

A small sandy landing beside the parking area is the place to launch your canoe or kayak. Ross Mountain rises directly across the lake, and Mount Blue is to the left. The majority of the state-owned shoreline is to the left of the landing. You do not have to go far to encounter the stumps, many of which lie just below the surface and can be difficult to spot. The lake narrows along its midsection, and then widens again at its southern end.

Although not remote at all, this bay has a good sense of seclusion. This is the best spot to see the large bald patch on the side of Mount Blue, like a toupee that has slipped from position. Stumps rise from the water in grotesque patterns. The southernmost campsite is only a 1.2-mile paddle from the parking area.

Garnet Lake, with its shallow waters and moderate elevation of 1,470 feet, features a warmwater fishery of perch, bullhead, bass, and pike. If you are looking for a side adventure to fill your time here, the hike to Lizard Pond comes highly recommended. The remote, boat-access-only campsite is found on the west shore, with a trail that climbs 260 feet in 1.3 miles to an attractive lean-to on the southern shore.

24 Thirteenth Lake

Synopsis: Enjoy a canoe-camping adventure amid the gem-studded "Garnet Hills"
Paddling Distance: 50 feet to 2 miles
Number of Campsites: 13

A better candidate for the name "Garnet Lake" would be Thirteenth Lake at the northern end of the Siamese Ponds Wilderness. Not only can garnets still be found in small quantities in many of the surrounding mountains, but one garnet mine remains in active service just outside the wilderness boundaries. You'll pass the mine's driveway as you head to the lake.

The earliest garnet mine was opened on the slopes of nearby Gore Mountain in 1878, and this would eventually supplant logging as the region's dominant industry. Frank Hooper started a new mine on Ruby Mountain in 1893 but expanded to a much larger site in 1908. Located in the hills above Thirteenth Lake, this operation employed roughly 100 people, many of whom lived in a small community of company-owned buildings nearby. This mine exhausted its ore supply in 1928, although it still exists as a curious (though less-than-pristine) site on state land. One of the company's log buildings survives as Garnet Hill Lodge, visible from the lake.

Thirteenth Lake's name has nothing to do with this industrial past. Instead, its origins surface from an even deeper part of Adirondack history, when an eighteenth-century land purchase was subdivided into numbered townships; Thirteenth Lake happened to be the largest body of water in Township 13, a diamond-shaped tract that also included much of the East Branch Sacandaga River. The lake has been a destination for sportsmen since the nineteenth century when a succession of lodges operated on or near its shores, including Bennett's Sportsman's Retreat, John Reed's Maple Cottage, Henry Maxam's Thirteenth Lake House, and John Wade's Thirteenth Lake Lodge.

Today, the entire lake is owned by the state except for one small section on the east shore, where a homeowners' association maintains a private boat launch and beach. Public access is found at the north end

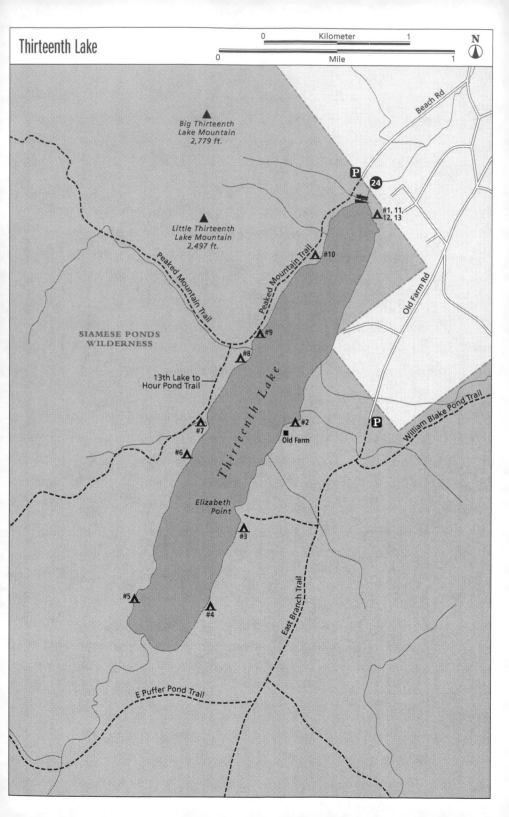

of the lake, where there is a cluster of walk-in campsites near another small beach. Several primitive campsites are scattered along the shoreline, making this a prime spot for an overnight adventure.

Getting There

Access to this part of the Siamese Ponds Wilderness—which has much to offer in addition to Thirteenth Lake—begins on Thirteenth Lake Road. This paved byway starts on NY 28 in North River and traces a winding course through Christian Hill and alongside Thirteenth Brook. At 3.3 miles you reach a junction with Beach Road, the gravel spur that leads in 0.6 miles to the large trailhead parking area at the end of the road, just a few hundred feet from Thirteenth Lake.

The Lake

From the parking area at the end of Beach Road, a short trail leads in 450 feet to a small beach, where canoes can be launched. This path is graded for universal accessibility, with four walk-in campsites and a picnic area nearby. As you might expect, an area so easy to reach is quite popular through the warmer months, and these first campsites are occupied most summer weekends.

Boats can be hand-launched at the beach. The lake is 2 miles long and a half mile wide, and it offers several hours' worth of paddling. Most of the primitive campsites are found on the west shore, which has no shortage of rocky ledges. However, all the best views are on the east shore, where you have prime views of the range of small mountains that rise as much as 1,100 feet above the lake. One of the most popular destinations is Elizabeth Point, a spacious campsite located on a short peninsula along the lake's southeast quadrant, 1.4 miles from the launching point. It offers good swimming and great views, but it is so popular that it is not recommended for anyone in search of solitude.

If your intent is to fish, note that there are some special regulations that apply to the lake. Only artificial lures are permitted, with daily limits of five trout per day (any size) and three landlocked salmon (15 inches or larger only).

Thirteenth Lake at Elizabeth Point. *Photo courtesy of the author*

Thirteenth Lake is nearly surrounded by the Siamese Ponds Wilderness, but its waters are exempt from the motorless requirement because of the lake's shared ownership. The Garnet Hill Property Owners Association maintains a private beach and boat launch on the east shore.

Motorboats are not banned, but they are restricted to electric motors only. Since the public launch requires a 450-foot walk to the water from the Beach Road trailhead, most of the boats on the lake tend to be canoes and kayaks.

Swimming is popular at Thirteenth Lake, but leeches are present.

This is undoubtedly one of the more attractive water bodies in the Adirondacks, with its mountain views and undeveloped shoreline. Several varieties of trout share the waters, and loons often patrol the surface near the beach. Although not remote like a true backcountry destination—portions of the Garnet Hill development are plainly visible from most of the lake—there is no doubting its wildness. Perhaps one of the greatest joys of the lake is its view southwest toward the mountainous heart of the wilderness, which may beckon you on to further adventures.

25 Henderson Lake

Synopsis: Prepare to be awed by the mountain views
Paddling Distance: 0.3 to 1.3 miles
Number of Campsites: 4, including one lean-to

Henderson Lake is effectively the start of the Hudson River, although if you're new to the Adirondacks the version of that mighty river you'll encounter here will be unlike any preconceived notion you might possess. At this northerly latitude, the river is more of a glorified mountain stream, bearing little resemblance to the urban river seen off Manhattan's West Side. Instead of skyscrapers, expect to feel humbled by towering mountains. And instead of busy street traffic, be prepared for the wide-open spaces of the Northeast's largest protected wilderness.

Henderson is an artificial lake that was not added to the Forest Preserve until 2003—meaning that, as this region grew in popularity through the twentieth century, it remained off-limits to the public for most of that period. Experiencing the lake today, that may seem difficult to believe; aside from the earthen dam itself, the lake presents itself as a wild body of water, as scenic as any national park.

Earlier in this book I wrote about the backpacking trip to Duck Hole, which passes Henderson Lake and starts at the same trailhead. This is more than just a parking area in the woods; as you'll see when you arrive, this is a major historic site, now preserved and interpreted for the benefit of those hikers not in a rush to reach the backcountry.

The history of Upper Works is well documented and has been retold numerous times. In a nutshell, this was the site of a remote iron mine first scouted in 1826 and developed a few years later. One of the principals was named David Henderson, who died in 1845 during a hunting accident at the spot known ever since as Calamity Pond. The original mine struggled to turn a profit, however, due to its remote location and the enormous costs of transporting the ore out of the mountains.

In 1901, the site played a role in national history when Vice President Theodore Roosevelt vacationed here. While his family was staying in the yellow building that now stands next to the modern parking area,

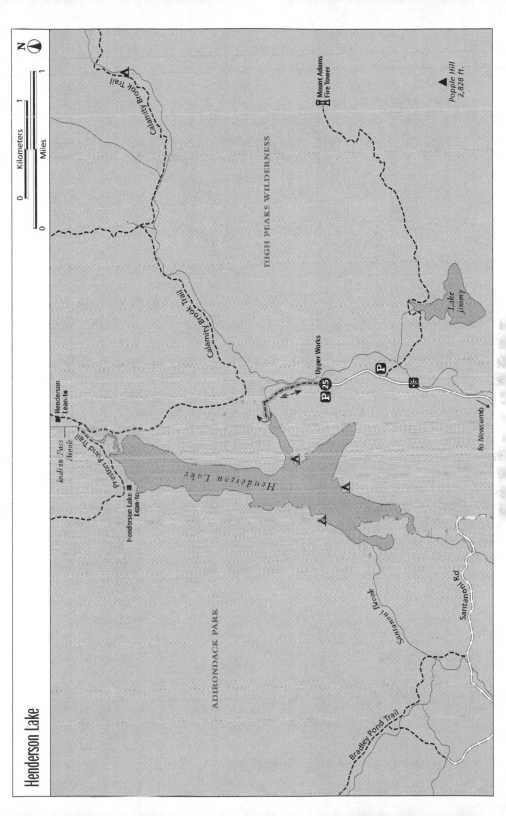

Roosevelt was camping at Lake Tear of the Clouds, high on the shoulder of Mount Marcy. The president had been shot the week before, and although he was originally expected to recover, messengers rushed into the wilderness with news: William McKinley was now near death. Roosevelt rushed out of the woods, but by the time he reached North Creek he learned of the president's passing moments before.

During World War II, the old mine was revived and expanded when titanium was discovered in large quantities. This operation reshaped not just the immediate landscape but also a section of the Hudson River. The giant tailing piles are still plainly evident as you drive to Upper Works, and gravel sourced from the remnants of the Tahawus Mine are now ubiquitous—forming the bed of the road, a portion of the hiking trail, and even the Henderson Lake dam itself.

Getting There

From Northway (Interstate 87) Exit 29, drive west on Blue Ridge Road (also called Boreas Road) for 17 miles to the right turn for Tahawus. Follow this road, CR 25, to a fork at 6.3 miles. Turn left and continue to a series of three parking areas: Santanoni at 8.2 miles, East River at 9.2, and the Upper Works parking area at the end of the road, 9.5 miles from Blue Ridge Road. The trail to Henderson Lake begins at Upper Works at the end of the road. The parking area is surrounded by the Upper Works historical site.

The Lake

Reaching Henderson Lake entails a carry of about 0.5 miles, all of it along a closed gravel road amenable to canoe carts. The journey begins in the abandoned village of Adirondac, now a collection of picturesque chimneys and cellar foundations. The MacNaughton Cottage, built in 1834, is the only surviving structure; the rest collapsed under heavy snows shortly before the Open Space Institute acquired the property in 2003. Not all of the structures here were equally old, but all have a story to tell. Today the former road through the village is a promenade lined with rail fences and interpretive signs.

Henderson Lake. *Photo courtesy of the author*

At 0.2 miles you reach the register station, located at the original (and much more modest) public parking area, now a revegetation area. The old road narrows as it enters the woods, but it remains a gravel-surfaced road. At 0.4 miles, you cross a bridge over a stream that, despite its humble appearance, is the start of the Hudson River.

Turn left at the junction just beyond the bridge and reach Henderson Lake's dam 500 feet later, made out of the same dull gray crushed rock as the road surface. Don't be worried if your first impression of the lake is underwhelming; all you can see here is one narrow arm, not the main show. A gravel landing beside the dam provides plenty of room to launch canoes, and a 0.3-mile paddle up the arm brings you to the lake's central north–south axis.

There are mountains in every direction! To the west is Henderson Mountain, dwarfed by Santanoni Peak behind it, identifiable by the rockslide scar just below the summit, resembling a tautly pulled necktie. Mount Andrew is the prominent peak to the southwest, with Adams, Calamity, and the flanks of the MacIntyre Range to the east. The outlet channel is aimed like a gunsight on Mount Colden, while MacNaughton Mountain dominates the northern horizon. But the biggest stunner of all is Wallface with its precipitous cliffs—the Adirondacks' rugged answer to Yosemite.

There are four camping options at Henderson Lake, including a lean-to at the north end and three tent sites scattered along the southern reaches. The first site is just 0.3 miles from the dam, on the south shore right where the channel opens onto the main lake; the most distant site is the lean-to, which is also accessible by trail. The rugged shoreline, with its plunging rock ledges, doesn't provide too many other options.

Henderson is often beset by northerly winds, as evidenced by the patterns of driftwood pushed into some of the southernmost bays. On a gusty day, the lake may be whipped up into whitecaps that could be unsafe for smaller canoes. The lake is deep, and the steep shoreline is almost inaccessible in a few spots.

But in calm conditions there are only a few other lakes in the Adirondacks this scenic! Its artificial origins and long history of non-wilderness uses are all easily forgotten once out on the water.

AUTHOR'S NOTE

Many of the historical notes sprinkled throughout this book were drawn from my long career of writing about Adirondack Park and were not the result of any novel research. Much of this was information I found when writing the Discover the Adirondacks series, and other tidbits drawn from the body of common knowledge that any writer working in the region is expected to rattle off as a matter of course. In many other cases, I refer to events that have happened during my writing career, which has extended beyond guidebooks into topics of wilderness advocacy.

I urge readers with an interest in learning more about the Adirondacks' rich history to track down a copy of Frank Graham Jr.'s *The Adirondack Park: A Political History* (1978). If this accessible text leaves you hungry for more of the same, then I highly suggest any of the histories penned by Barbara McMartin. (The quality of Adirondack literature has been greatly diminished ever since her passing in 2005.)

It is difficult to write about the Oswegatchie River without resisting the temptation to cite Herbert F. Keith's 1972 classic *Man of the Woods*, a highly enjoyable treatise on the colorful guides who once operated in that area. This book is just one entry in an entire genre of Adirondack literature focusing (often with healthy doses of nostalgia) on the various personalities who once made a living throughout these woods. Sadly, many of the best of those titles have gone out of print.

My hypothesis in the introduction to this guidebook that the Adirondacks are the result of a "Hadean speedbump" comes from my own imagination. However, it was an idea inspired by John Dvorak's *How the Mountains Grew: A New Geological History of North America* (2021). Dvorak does mention how North America is rolling over the fragments of another lost continental plate, but he stops short of tying this information to the origins of the Adirondack Mountains; therefore, I took that last creative leap myself.

For my commentary on passenger pigeons in the Adirondacks, and their ecological history, I refer the reader to Charles C. Mann's *1491*

(2005), a magnificent depiction of what the Americas were probably like before Columbus sailed the ocean blue. Again, there is no specific reference in this book to Pigeon Lake, or even the Adirondacks, but the dots were easy to connect.

CAMPSITE INDEX